MW01194183

SAM'S THRONE

Including the Mt. Judea, Valley of the Blind,
Cave Creek and Rickett's Mountain areas.

ARKANSAS

by
Clay Frisbie

CHOCKSTONE PRESS, INC.
P.O. Box 1269
Conifer, CO 80433

Classic Rock Climbs: Sam's Throne, Arkansas

ISBN: 1-57540-025-1 *Classic Rock Climbs* series
   Sam's Throne, Arkansas

Published and distributed by:

Chockstone Press, Inc.
P.O. Box 1269
Conifer, Colorado 80433

In praise of God, who created the rocks to climb on, the Father of my lord Jesus Christ the second Adam.

ACKNOWLEDGMENTS

Many people helped with this guide. Sally, my wife, and three children Janie, Cally and Cassi, contributed inspiration and allowed me the time on the rock to glean the information for the guide. Special thanks to Tom Hancock for his extensive help and hours of work with the overview drawings and to Ladd Campbell for his hours of help in preparing photos. Also thanks to Sean Burns for his help with Cave Creek, to Stacy Fairbanks for his help with of the Fraggle Rock area and to James Carl Hefley for providing historical information. I would also like to extend my appreciation to my friends and fellow climbers who gave information and ideas to help with this guide.

Mark Bidford, Billy Bisswanger, Herbert and Grace Bolin, Cathy Collette, Mike Davison, Sandy Fleming, Eric Forney, Roderick Franklin, Delbert and Peggy Frisbie, Herb and Jackie Gates, Barry Gilbert, Kevin Hale, Jim Herschend, Tom Kacprowicz, Jim Karpowicz, Anthony Kostiulk, Tony Mayse, George Powell, Mike Stites, Craig Thomas, Linda Seehusen, Kevin Sosinavage and Sandre Wrede.

Finally I wish to thank Chuck Caughlin, Woody Delp, Tom Hancock, Bob Scheier, Chandler Schooler and Jon Von Canon who have been my friends and climbing partners over the last several years. Some of my most cherished memories in the vertical world have been spent with these guys sharing the sharp end of a rope, hundreds of times on different routes throughout northern Arkansas. Without their patience, guidance, inspiration and encouragement this guide would not have come into being.

PREFACE

The information in this guide could have been kept private so that only a select few could preserve the area for themselves. By making this information available to the public it will inevitably lead to greater use and impact on the area. As a user of this guide please take the responsibility to make a positive impact where you pass. Leave it a better place than you found it. The purpose of this guide is to communicate information so others may also enjoy the plethora of different routes these areas have to offer.

TABLE OF CONTENTS

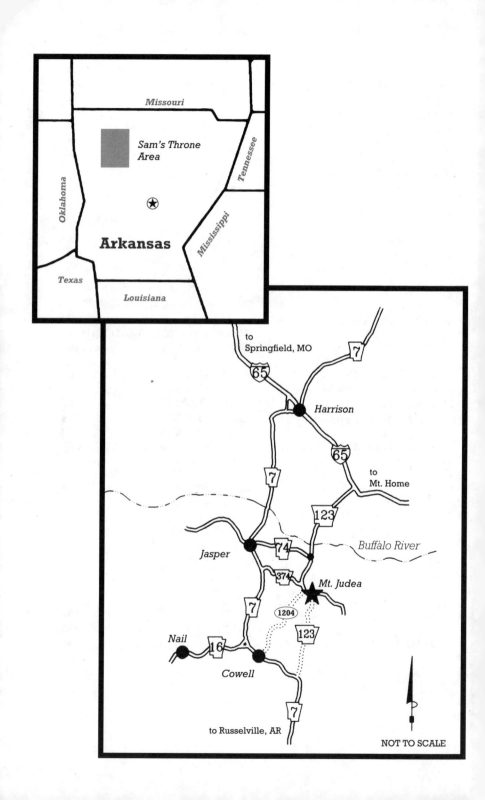

Missouri

Sam's Throne
Area

Oklahoma

Arkansas

Tennessee

Mississippi

Texas

Louisiana

to
Springfield, MO

65

7

Harrison

65

to
Mt. Home

7

123

Buffalo River

Jasper

74

374

Mt. Judea

7

1204

123

Nail

16

Cowell

7

to Russelville, AR

NOT TO SCALE

INTRODUCTION

SAM'S THRONE

Climbing at Sam's Throne can be a delightful and enjoyable experience. Situated in the Boston Mountain Range of northern Arkansas, Sam's Throne sits atop a worn mountain ridge overlooking the tree filled valleys below. Sam's Throne, with its sandstone bluffs and primitive environment, provides a welcome retreat for climbers seeking relief from the flatland blues.

Climbers should be polite and courteous to the locals of this area. I have heard many stories of climbers being assisted by the locals. Many of us that have experienced car trouble have been helped out by total strangers on several occasions. I believe people in this rural community know the principle of helping one another. It is refreshing in our day and time to find this kind of attitude. Many places do not welcome climbers and to get help is the exception, not the rule. We, the climbers, should reciprocate by being respectful to the people of this area and by keeping the area clean.

GETTING THERE   The closest major town is Harrison, Arkansas which is about forty five minutes from all the areas. Little Rock and Fayetteville, Arkansas and Springfield, Missouri are all with in three hours of Sam's Throne.

The introduction to each chapter of this guide describes how to get to the trailhead for the particular area. Hiking approaches to almost all the areas are under thirty minutes.

HISTORY   Sam Davis (whom Sam's Throne is named after) originally settled in this area around the 1820s and is believed to be the first white man to live here. Embarking from Mississippi, Sam was in search of his sister whom he thought was stolen by the Indians. He lost her trail in the Big Creek Valley, where he set up his homestead. Sam's homestead was located northwest of the Big Creek and Dry Creek junction. This junction can be seen from atop the Patio area on Sam's Throne.

Sam had a wife and one son living with him on the homestead. He also had slaves that worked for him which probably means Sam was a Confederate during the Civil War. When he was in his 60s, rumor has it that he was

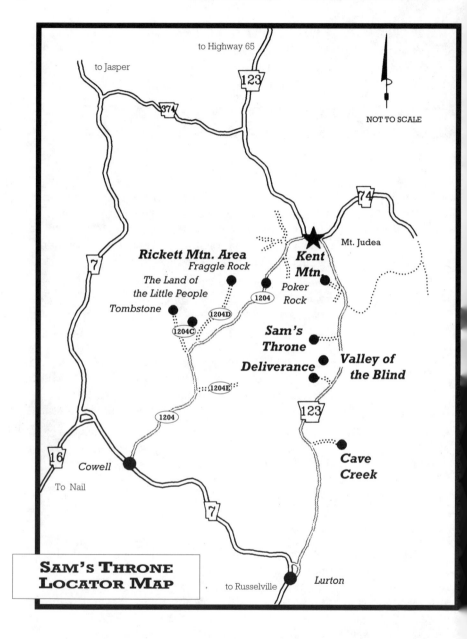

to Highway 65

to Jasper

123

374

7

NOT TO SCALE

74

Mt. Judea

★ Kent Mtn.

Rickett Mtn. Area
Fraggle Rock

*The Land of
the Little People*

Tombstone

Poker Rock

1204

1204D

1204C

Sam's Throne

Deliverance

**Valley of
the Blind**

1204E

1204

123

16

Cowell

To Nail

7

**Cave
Creek**

**SAM'S THRONE
LOCATOR MAP**

to Russelville

Lurton

wrestling a steer in the heat of the day. This generated a stroke that is theorized to have provoked his mental illness. Sam is believed to have phased in and out of his insanity. In the 1860 census, Sam Davis was found to be living with the Crinor family who Sam either gave or sold the land to. It was at this time of his life that his sanity came and went. During his later years, while living with the Crinor family, Sam would camp out for long periods on the mountain now known as Sam's Throne.

There are many colorful stories that surround Sam Davis. It is alleged he was a great buffalo hunter and was supposed to have killed the last buffalo in the valley. Some conjecture that the Buffalo River gets its name from the buffalo that roamed the area.

Another is about how Sam put up logs to block the walk up on Sam's Throne. There he is said to have barricaded himself in, hiding his gold. Of course, some say he was trying to make people think that was where he kept his gold, but that actually he kept his gold across the creek.

Sam was also known for preaching from on top the throne. He is said to have proclaimed that he was going to live for one thousand years. One thing to consider was that he was not preaching to an empty audience. Many people lived in the valley at this time. Whether they could understand or cared to understand what he was saying is another matter.

Sam had one son, Richard, who founded the town of Mt. Judea (pronounced "Judy"). After the Civil War, Richard was killed by some bushwhackers supposedly from Dover, Arkansas. Sam became consumed with bringing the killers to justice. Sam was last seen following their trail back to Dover and was never seen again.

The last private owners of the land that Sam's Throne is on were Mitchell Hefly and Willie Hefly. In the late 1930s the U.S. Government was in the process of buying up land in the area for the national forest. The land that Sam's Throne is on was thought to have been bought by the government in the late 1930s to the early 1940s.

Mt. Judea was a thriving rural area before World War II. It was after the war that people started to leave the area.

Although people have been visiting Sam's Throne for many years, technical rockclimbers began to patronize the area in the 1970s. Today Sam's has become a popular area for climbing because of its enchanting surroundings, easy approach and notable sandstone.

This whole area has always carried an air of mystery to outsiders due to its multicolored past. Stories about Civil War tragedies, family feuds, outlaws and hillbilly liquor have propagated this aura. It is not surprising that rockclimbers, notorious for their audacious nature, would patronize this area, only adding to the enigma that surrounds Sam's Throne.

For more information on the unique cultural history of Sam's Throne and the surrounding area read the book Way Back in the Hills *by James Carl Hefly (Living Books, Tyndale House Publishing, 1985).*

ENVIRONMENT AND WILDLIFE   Numerous types of animals inhabit the area. Black bears have been seen on rare occasions. Stories have circulated that bears have ripped apart tents searching for food. The black bears in this area are small and probably more afraid of you than you are of them. Bobcats have also been spotted in this area but never seem to bother anything other than one's sleep.

Insects are a different story altogether. This area is full of little parasites that love to make you itch and suffer. Chiggers and ticks are thick from May to October (until the first freeze). If these babies don't afflict you, maybe the man-eating horseflies will in August and September. Large, dousing quantities of bug juice can bring great relief and enjoyable climbing to those of you who are afflicted by the buzzing arthropods in spring and summer. Another insect that seems to infest this area from late summer to early fall is the walking stick. This prehistoric bug looks exactly like its name, a walking stick. Not to be concerned; this evil looking insect is interesting to observe and quite harmless.

Poisonous snakes do inhabit the area and are not necessarily a rare site to see. Snakes should not in anyway deter one from enjoying the harmoniousness of the surroundings. If the remote possibility does occur and you do come upon one of these creatures unexpectedly, leave it alone.

WHERE TO STAY   The closest developed camping area is Fairview Campgrounds. It is located three miles south of Lurton on Highway 7. Currently camping is free with developed campsites and running water available.

Many camp in the areas where they are climbing on National Forest lands, the most popular being Sam's Throne and Cave Creek. At both areas the campsites are undeveloped with no water or toilets available. As climbers and users of these areas it is up to us to keep them clean and maintain low impact policies:

- Pack out all toilet paper and human waste. At the least bury the waste six inches deep and carry out the toilet paper.
- Pack out all trash, whether it's yours or not.
- Do not cut down any trees. Bring in your own firewood or gather dead wood.

•   Digging is prohibited in archaeological sites.

Let's keep our crags clean and in as natural a state as possible. Please remember always to leave the area cleaner than you found it.

WEATHER   Any time you can find to get away is a good time, because year-round climbing can be obtained at Sam's Throne. The most comfortable seasons for climbing at Sam's Throne are fall and spring when the temperatures are ideal. It is at this time of year that the air is cool and the bugs are dead (thank God). In the summer, bliss can be acquired by climbing on the north-facing walls or by taking an afternoon plunge in the Buffalo River. In the winter, temperatures can vary wildly, from shorts and T-shirt weather to perfect ice climbing conditions. When the temperature drops, pleasant climbing can be found on the south-facing walls of the East Bluff, The Throne, Cave Creek and Valley of the Blind.

GEOLOGY   Atoka Sandstone: This hard sandstone provides for widely varied and enjoyable climbing.

WHY CLIMB?   Although many sports offer physical challenges, few demand as much inner strength as climbing. There is a constant personal search, an advanced form of mind control, to fight doubt and focus on the task at hand. The challenge is within yourself. Like few other sports, the climber selects the route and chooses the problem to solve, choosing the difficulty or challenge that one wants to confront. Can you recognize the moves? Can you select the right sequence? Can you execute it? If not, are you prepared for the consequences? At every grade, it is the same; a climber selects the problems within their own limits, or well below them, and so makes up his or her own game. The deeper you delve into the mysteries of climbing, the deeper you delve into your own mind. What makes climbing extraordinary is that there are no rules other than the ones the climber imposes upon him or herself.

EQUIPMENT   A standard rack might consist of wired chocks, active cam units, tri-cams and full length runners.

The most important consideration for equipment in this area is that various placements are found in horizontal cracks. Active camming units with flexible cables and tri-cams seem to provide the best protection for horizontal crack placements. Small tri-cams work great for the shallow crack placements and small pockets which incorporate a numerous amount of the protection at Sam's Throne. Also, full length (twenty-four inch) runners come in handy for tying off chickenheads and jugs, which on some routes is the only means of protection available.

ETHICS   Since all the climbs at Sam's Throne can quite easily be top roped, ethics in the area have been held in high regard. Lead climbing is considered an art. As in music, a lead climber uses his body like an instrument. Art is a way in which one can express one's self. Any ascent, whether the first or not, is a creation in several ways; the way in which the leader contorts his body to move upwards, choice of holds, means of resting and conserving one's strength, choice of protection and the skills used in placing the protection. As a lead climber fashions a route up the rock, the boldness to climb on or the discipline to stop and protect make up part of the creation of the route itself. Not only the gymnastic moves, but also the mind game of artful protection make for the brilliant creativity of a route that can be enjoyed and experienced by all. So we honor the first ascentionist and climb the routes as they were originally done leaving the creative effort intact. Never—ever—add or remove fixed anchors on an existing route!

With all that aside, free climbing with hand-placed and natural protection is the general rule. The character of the rock is such that it usually lends itself well to hand-placed protection. As a result, there is very little fixed protection. Hanging out on a steep face might become a physically demanding labor.

Sam's Throne certainly does not have the large walls of Yosemite or of other climbing areas out West, but with its short climbs, Sam's Throne does have its own unique, challenging lead climbing.

STYLE   All the routes listed in this guide are red point climbs with the exception of a few routes which are top-ropes (TR) or boulder problems (BP). Free climbing with hand-placed and natural protection is the general rule. Listed below are terms different terms used for styles of ascent.

boulder problem (BP) A short climb usually under thirty feet that is normally free climbed without a belay or a rope for protection.

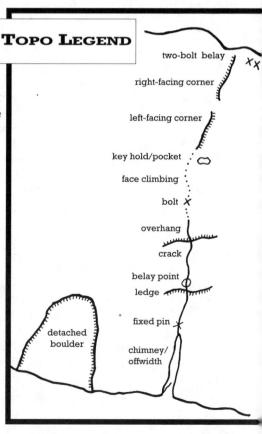

TOPO LEGEND

two-bolt belay
right-facing corner
left-facing corner
key hold/pocket
face climbing
bolt
overhang
crack
belay point
ledge
detached boulder
fixed pin
chimney/ offwidth

top-roping (TR) Nothing wrong with this perfectly legitimate form of ascent. Just do not fool yourself into thinking that you have led a climb if you have top-roped a route.

ground up A style of lead ascent on a route; to climb a route with out top-roping or rappelling down to preview the route or other shenanigans like that. The route is climbed from bottom to top, any gear or fixed protection that is placed must be done while leading, as opposed to on rappel or top rope.

flash Free climbing a route from bottom to top on first attempt without falling or weighting the rope—be it top-rope or led. (Sorry you only get one chance to personally flash each given route per lifetime!) On-sight is just another way of saying flash with out any detailed knowledge of the climb.

pink point A successful, no falls or weighting of the rope, bottom to top free climbing lead ascent of a given route. The protection is pre-fixed before leading such as rappelling down and fixing gear or lowering off a lead climb then re-leading the route without removing the pieces. When referring to bolts, the runners are already clipped and in place. This is usually considered bad style. Pink point is sometimes used as a way to practice lead climbing, or finish leading a route to be able to later red point the route.

red point A successful no fall or weighting of the rope, bottom to top free climbing lead ascent of a given route. All protection that is placed is put in on-lead. A route may be attempted many times before a successful red point is attained.

RATINGS The Yosemite Decimal System is used for all rock climbs in this guide. A subgrading system is used to further delineate between the "easiest" and the "hardest" for climbs 5.10 and harder. The upper rock climbing grades may show an a, b, c, or d suffix for sport climbs. For traditional and mixed routes a + and − suffix further defines the difficulty. The decimal ratings are the standard by which climbs are compared. The following are examples:

Sport Traditional and Mixed
5.10a = 5.10−
5.10b/c = 5.10
5.10d = 5.10+

A route that is normally top-roped is indicated with the letters TR. A route that is normally climbed as a boulder problem is indicated with the letters BP. The overall grade assigned to a climb is a reflection of the hardest move encountered, unless a lengthy succession of difficult moves warrants a higher grade. Steep routes are notorious for pumping up or flaming the forearms which means having to protect the route takes more time, making the route much more difficult than simple top-roping. The vast majority of routes have been rated on a lead basis. For the steep, hard-to-protect, time-consuming leads, this means the ratings may vary compared to top-roping. Many of the difficult routes have seen only one or two ascents in some of the less popular areas. Rating the difficulty of a climb is highly subjective. Disagreements on ratings may arise due to the varying abilities of the climbers who rate them. The only guarantee of accuracy in this guide is if you are five-foot-six-inches tall, male, weigh 140 pounds with a deformed left heel and prefer climbing cracks on sunny 60° days with relatively low humidity and your first name starts with a "c" and ends with a "y." The purpose of rating routes is not to over rate, thereby inflating egos, or under rate, thereby sandbagging, others that follow. The purpose of rating routes is to estimate the difficulties and challenges a route provides. This is to assist climbers to decide for themselves if an adventure is one that they are capable of.

Aid climbing; advancing up the wall by hanging from one piece of protection to another piece, is a common practice used to climb big walls. The common grading system of aid climbing ranges from A0, easy fixed pieces, to A5, the most difficult aid.

STAR RATINGS   A star system is employed to designate route quality. It ranges from mediocre climbs, having no stars, up to superb, four-star climbs. Many things make for a quality route such as the protection available, sustained climbing for the grade, or the aesthetic look or run of the line. This star system is very subjective. To the author's point of view, good cracks and weird offwidths climbs are almost always good for an extra star. Since we are talking subjective, that would probably mean any first ascent by the author is liable to have an extra star. I would like to stress that many of the quality lines are not in perfect condition. Many have some loose rock, or some may have lichen, moss and cobwebs to the point that it may interfere with climbing. The one quality that most of these routes do have in common is superb adventure on the sharp end of the rope.

DANGER RATING   Further ratings are given to alert the climber as to the serious potential fall. The potential danger ratings PG, S, VS and X are listed along with the rating to alert climbers to the possible risk of certain routes. In an area where most of the routes are traditional, I believe it is only fair to give as much information as feasible, information that could help make an on-sight lead more viable for subsequent climbers. First, almost every route in this guide that has a rating with a PG, S or X was done ground up without a top-rope or inspecting on rappel before leading the route. Especially on traditional routes, advanced familiarity with the moves and foreknowledge of the route certainly distract from the boldness and the ability required to climb a route on-sight (which certainly takes away any credit for boldness which would ordinarily be due). Without debate, ground up is the most respected style in which to establish new routes or repeat old ones.

To rap down and pre-inspect or rehearse moves before leading a route dishonors those who attempt to repeat a route in good style. It could certainly be said that a first ascent done in this style is not a true first ascent. To top-rope a potentially serious route and then led it without letting others know this was the style of ascent could potentially leave other climbers hopelessly sandbagged. In this guide, less then half a dozen routes were done in this style. On these few routes, I have written notes in the route description to alert or suggest wisdom in top-roping these few routes first.

These ratings assume that a competent climber has rigged the climb with the best protection possible and is climbing solid at that level of difficulty. Climbs receiving no protection ratings are generally thought of as "safe" for competent leaders; however, most injuries occur on those climbs that are "well protected". Runout sections that are relatively easy compared to the overall grade of the climb are not always noted. With the recent trend toward extremely well protected routes, one still might find some of the routes without ratings slightly exhilarating. This is meant only as a guide, for once on the rock the climber assumes all responsibility for his or her safety.

PG   Protection is usually adequate but a bit sporty. A potential for a fifteen-foot fall with the possibility of a bad injury because of inadequate or unavailable protection.

S   A serious potential for ground fall because of inadequate or unavailable protection.

X   A very serious potential for ground fall because of inadequate or unavailable protection at the crux sections and should be considered more as a free solo than a lead. The best protection is your own climbing ability and experience.

FIXED PROTECTION   As new routes are bolted, fixed protection issues need to be weighed and tempered by aesthetic awareness and a sense of appreciation for our finite resource, the rock. The bolt, it has been said, is the great equalizer. It's presence removes the element of danger.

The set method for bolting in the Sam's Throne traditional areas (West Bluff, East Bluff, Hero Maker, The Throne) has been to do it on lead. Rappel or top-rope bolting practices are not welcome in these areas. If the bolt cannot be placed on lead, maybe the climb needs to stay a top rope. The reason for this practice where natural lines abound, has been to make bolting inordinately more arduous, requiring more commitment to the route. This has served as a spontaneous inherent means to manage and/or limit bolting in these traditional areas.

Generally, in all the other areas, there is no set method of bolting that is held sacred. Of course, one can always climb in better style than the prevailing ethic. Though many recent climbs have been bolted on the lead, perhaps as many have been done via top-rope or rappel. Thus the so called "European Style" has taken root in these areas, but this is not to ignore the fact that some climbers disdain the pre-engineering of new routes and proliferation of bolts. Unfortunately, in the mental confusion resulting from the imposition of new ideas and methods, a *very* few persons during the early '90s determined to rid the area of certain routes. In *Climbing* magazine (Issue #102), editor Michael Kennedy illuminates with keen insight that "a hole is a hole, whether filled with steel or epoxy." Bolt chopping as a means of deterring bolting is not effective unless it is supported by a *vast majority* of local climbers. At Sam's this has not been the case. The chopping of a bolt can do more damage to the rock than did the drilling of the original hole. Also, chopped bolts tend to be replaced. Instead of promoting our egos, let us promote the enjoyment of rock climbing.

Routes created via rappel and top-rope offer a great deal of discretion as to where they lie and as to the position and quantity of fixed protection. To all but the first ascent party, a bolt is a bolt, whether installed on the way up, or on the way down. It is much more important that fixed protection be placed in effective positions on routes of sufficient quality and safety as to be of interest to climbers after the first ascent. Built-in ground falls and long runouts on difficult terrain are absurdities on routes that have been rehearsed on top-rope and/or preprotected. This situation leaves other climbers hopelessly sandbagged. For routes that have not been led on-sight or from ground up, it demonstrates much better perspective and integrity to create routes that can be reasonably led on-sight.

At this time, the choices for bolts seem to be expansion bolts such as Rawl or Metolius. The bolts should be ⅜" to ½" in diameter and at least three inches in length. All bolts and anchors should be painted to match the color of the rock. With a vision to the future, inferior hardware and shoddy craftsmanship should not be tolerated. As time passes it is hoped that climbers experienced in the placement of pitons and bolts will take the initiative to maintain or correct fixed protection that has deteriorated or is no longer safe due to the effects of time, environment or repeated use. The purpose of rock climbing is to enjoy oneself on the rock, not die from the failure of an anchor or fixed pin.

FIRST ASCENTS   A first ascent requires leading a route (belayed from below). Generally, the person whose name appears first led the crux of the route originally. First ascents are listed after each route with **FA** for first ascent (aid climb, even slight use of aid) and **FFA** for first free ascent. A new route FFA is completed when the leader starts at the bottom of the cliff and climbs to the top, without falling, grabbing slings or hanging on the rope (red point).

The origins of many routes were never kept. When dealing with a closed-mouth group of people that climb independently for their own personal satisfaction, obtaining "who did what" has been hard to establish. This information was compiled from personal experience and from other climbers who patronize the area. I perceive that there may be many climbers that have not received credit for first ascents, especially those prior to 1980 and I can only apologize and ask to be notified to make corrections. There is also the possibility that the Native Americans who lived in this area might have procured some first ascents that we will never know about. This sandstone is about two-hundred-and-thirty-million-years-old, give or take a few years. I am sure there are mistakes on FAs and FFAs.

Tradition holds that the first ascentionist is to give the route a name. This route, that now has a name, can be distinguished from other routes by use of the name. For example, instead of saying "Yeah! You know that great climb. It's on the white face. A thin crack left-facing dihedral on that wall around the corner from that other great climb." Instead you can say "Mike's Crack 5.10–" to communicate the route.

SUPPLIES   For those wanting good company and hot food, Herb's Restaurant in Mt. Judea provides an excellent refuge. Herbert and Grace Bolin, the owners, have been in business since 1985 and have always welcomed climbers. Besides good food and a welcome retreat from camp cooking, one might catch up on the latest climbing gossip. They also stock a few climbing necessities such as tape and chalk.

LOCAL CLIMBING SHOPS

Pack Rat
2397 Green Acres
Fayetteville, AR 72703
(501)582-2558

Take a Hike
911 E. Broadway
Little Rock, AR 72211

Ozark Cliff Hangers Climbing Gym
1202 Eagle Crest
Nixa, MO
(417)725-0280

LOCAL GUIDE SERVICES

Petra Climbing
1367 E. Dunkirk
Springfield MO 65804
(417)881-1141 or (417)889-5904

EMERGENCY NUMBERS

Newton County Sheriff's Dept.
Jasper, AR
(501)446-5124

National Forest Department
Jasper, AR
(501)446-2228

North Arkansas Medical Center
Harrison, AR
(501)365-2000

Mark Wilford and Clay Frisbie on the first ascent of All-Star Wrestling (5.12–) ★★★★, Mt. Judea, House of His Healing Presence

CHAPTER ONE

KENT MOUNTAIN

Kent Mountain is the knob of rock that lies on the west side of the road just after the switchbacks end when coming up the hill from the town of Mount Judea. This is a small area with short walls and good clean rock. It lies on unfriendly private land, so the information on routes here is meant as historic information only.

Do not climb at Kent Mountain unless you have the expressed permission from the landowner. If you climb there without it, you very well might end up with a load of buck shot fired at your backside.

1   **Peeping Tom (11 A2+) ★★★**   Right of *Shaved Pussy,* facing east is a corridor or cave. A crack system runs up out of the cave. Climb up ten feet to where the thin crack system starts. Hard moves lead up (5.11) to a fixed pin. Follow the crack system up right to the roof. At the roof begin aid climbing the thin seam under the roof. Tied-off thin knifeblades work pretty good in this seam. After aiding past the roof the crack begins again with 5.10 climbing. 50 feet. FFA: Clay Frisbie/Mike Stites 1991.

2   **Shaved Pussy (10–) ★★★★**   Located on the east side of Kent Mountain where the rock wall has separated to create a small canyon. Striking straight-in crack on orange rock that starts as a handcrack and diminishes to a fingercrack near the top. This sustained route is well worth the hike up to Kent Mountain even if it is the only climb you do here. [The first ascent of this climb was determined by who could be the first to reach the climb. The day before Mike Stites, Mike Davidson, Tom Karpowitz and Randy Schell scouted out the Kent Mountain area. When I arrived at their campfire that night they were talking about this new secret area that had a spectacular route with a straight-in crack—a true jewel. They were talking about putting a blindfold on anyone they took there to keep the area a secret at least until all the good natural lines had been done. The next morning everyone made a mad dash from the cars to the base of the climb because everybody wanted the first lead of the spectacular new line. Stites was the

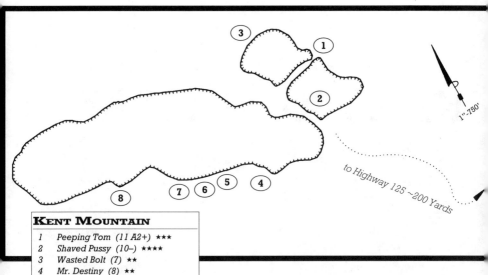

KENT MOUNTAIN

1	*Peeping Tom (11 A2+)* ★★★
2	*Shaved Pussy (10–)* ★★★★
3	*Wasted Bolt (7)* ★★
4	*Mr. Destiny (8)* ★★
5	*The Nose (10)* ★★
6	*Break Dancing (12a)* ★★★
7	*Wet Down Under (8)* ★★★
8	*Possum Kingdom (10c)* ★★★

first one there and made quick work of snatching the first ascent. This route was every bit as good as we anticipated.] 55 feet. FFA: Mike Stites/Randy Schell, 1991.

3 **Wasted Bolt (7)** ★★   On the west side of detached boulder, friction and edge up low-angle slab past one bolt to top. 40 feet.

4 **Mr. Destiny (8)** ★★   A handcrack in a right-facing dihedral. The dihedral angles left turning into an offwidth at the top. 30 feet.

5 **The Nose (10)** ★★   Right-facing thin dihedral crack. 30 feet.

6 **Break Dancing (12a)** ★★★   Left-facing dihedral with three bolts. Boulder problem start makes for the crux of the route. A good spotter helps. The upper part of this route has not been completed. Unless this area becomes more congenial, it probably won't. FA: Frisbie/Stites 1992 (not finished).

7 **Wet Down Under (8)** ★★★   A roof crack that turns into a striking handcrack runs straight up with jugs along the crack. To start climb up ten feet to where crack begins as a offwidth with a short roof. 50 feet. FFA: Tom Karpowitz/Mike Davidson 1991.

8 **Possum Kingdom (10c)** ★★★   Left of walkup, clean face with a pin and four bolts. Two-bolt anchor. 45 feet. FFA: Sean Burns.

9 **Barracuda (10a TR)** ★★   Ten feet left of *Possum Kingdom* and five feet right of arête, start on the sharp fingerholds.

10   **G-Spot (12b)** ★★   Thirty feet around the corner from *Possum Kingdom* is an orange face with four bolts, two-bolt anchor on the top. 45 feet. FFA: Sean Burns.

11   **Impotent (11+)** ★★★   Short, blank, white face with one bolt halfway up the wall. This route may be short, but it is full of hard, sequential, balancey moves. I originally hoped this route could be done as a boulder problem without top-roping the route first. After taking over thirty long falls while trying to approach this route as a boulder problem over several different occasions, I ended up with a miserable groin injury that took over a year to heal. After that, I decided it was time to break out the rope. One bolt and tri-cams might come in handy. 35 feet. FFA: Frisbie/Hancock/Stites 1991.

Tom Hancock on Shaved Pussy (5.10–) ★★★★, ***Kent Mountain. Photo: Woody Delp.***

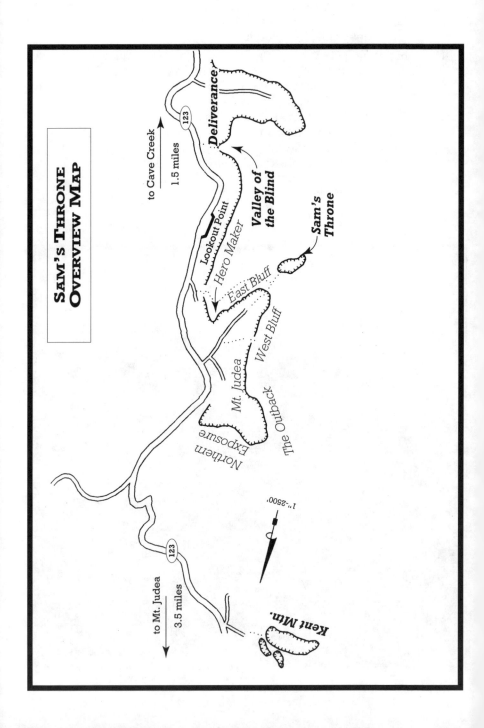

Sam's Throne
Overview Map

to Cave Creek
1.5 miles

123

Deliverance

Lookout Point

Hero Maker

Valley of
the Blind

East Bluff

Sam's
Throne

West Bluff

Mt. Judea

The Outback

Northern
Exposure

1"=2500'

123

to Mt. Judea
3.5 miles

Kent Mtn.

CHAPTER TWO

SAM'S THRONE (MT. JUDEA)

Mt. Judea (pronounced "Mount Judy") is the worn mountaintop many refer to as Sam's Throne. This area is where most people currently camp. Mt. Judea encompasses the areas: Northern Exposure, The Outback, West Bluff, Main Bluff, East Bluff, Hero Maker and The Throne. It is an expanse of rock which covers about four miles of bluff line. It contains one of the largest unbroken cliff lines in Northern Arkansas with over two hundred established routes. Mt. Judea has an abundance of routes over seventy feet high, and contains an extremely high concentration of traditional lead routes. Of the few routes that do have bolts, the vast majority are one- or two-bolt wonder mixed climbs that also require hand-placed gear. Along nearly all the bluff line on Mt. Judea one can find a natural line occurring about every 20 to 40 feet ranging from 5.7 to 5.10+ in difficulty. The vast majority of routes are steep and overhung with cracks mixed throughout. There are also some delicate face and slab routes spaced here and there. The climbing is good year round with tree shaded areas in the summer and many sun bathed bluffs in the winter.

NORTHERN EXPOSURE

The Northern Exposure area starts at Highway 123 and runs to the end of The Outback at the route Frog Hair on Mount Judea . It can be approached from either the end of the bluff at Highway 123 one-half mile north of the entrance to Sam's Throne by following the undeveloped bluff line for about a mile, or from any of the Outback walkdowns. I would recommend any approach from The Outback because it is closest to all the developed routes in Northern Exposure. Northern Exposure is one of the longer approaches at Sam's Throne; although thirty-minutes for an approach is not long. This area has, as the name suggests, north-facing walls. Climbing is good year round, except in the winter. In northern Arkansas, sandstone bluff lines that receive little or no sunlight are often covered with lichen and moss. In some places this poses no problem and in other places it can make the climbing much harder, especially on wet or humid days. Northern Exposure has more than its fair share of lichen and moss. Most of the developed routes are slightly dirty but well worth climbing, offering some excellent adventure routes. Only the smallest holds are affected by lichen and moss. Don't clean indiscriminately. Rather, respect the plant life and preserve the natural beauty and diversity.

1   **Twinkle Toes (11–)** ★★★★   Severely overhung offwidth fistcrack leads to a twenty-foot handcrack. A small vertical crack (which is not easy to spot, but very helpful) is located on the inside of the offwidth, which helps for the bouldery start. Very sustained climbing through roof leads to car-size chockstone death block stuck at the top of the route. The block is very much stuck in place (thank God!). Climb under, behind, around and on top of the block to top out. This is a great adventure climb for those who enjoy overhung handcrack climbing. This is a typical north-facing wall. Be ready to eat a little moss and lichen. This is an excellent route, well worth the walk. A little moss and lichen might be just what you need in your diet! 60 feet. FFA: Clay Frisbie/Tom Hancock 6/94.

2   **Octane Boost (11+)**   Located in a thirty-foot cave. Start on a thin crack located halfway back in the cave on the left side. Take the thin crack up rotten rock to gain access to the long roof crack. Locker handjams in the roof crack lead out fifteen feet to the lip of the roof. Pull on mossy holds and slither up the moss covered offwidth. This is by no means a nice clean route but a good place to get upside down for a bit. 50 feet. FFA: Clay Frisbie/Tom Hancock 6/94.

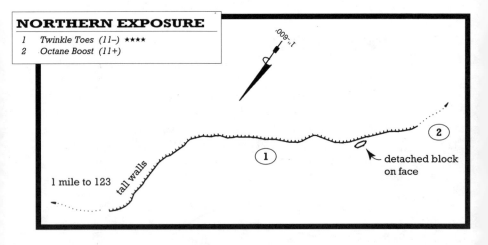

NORTHERN EXPOSURE

1   *Twinkle Toes (11–)* ★★★★
2   *Octane Boost (11+)*

1,600"

2

1

detached block
on face

1 mile to 123   tall walls

3   **Fatal Attraction (11–)** ★★★★ Striking right-facing dihedral (5.9) leads to a block-shaped roof with a thin right-facing dihedral crack above. This pronounced line provides superb climbing with good protection. Of course, the thin crack at the top (5.11–) is a suitable place to find out how well RPs or very small nuts work in sandstone! 70 feet. FFA: Clay Frisbie/Jon Von Canon 1990.

4   **Toxic Shock (A2+)** ★★★ Thin crack line right of *Fatal Attraction* that bisects the steep face. This route was originally done during a pouring rain storm. 60 feet. FFA: Mark Bidford 1995.

5   **Bones & Steel (8)** ★★★ Large right-facing flake. (Well, I guess it is not really a flake, but you know what I mean.) The first fifteen feet provide excellent handcrack. Continue up and to the right with face climbing. 55 feet. FFA: Woody Delp 1991.

6   **User Friendly (9)** ★★★★ This conspicuous line is surrounded by brown streaks on either side of a thin left-facing dihedral crack on a low-angle wall. This one is bound to be a classic, with several nonpumpy 5.9 moves on excellent rock. Great route to use those RPs on. 60 feet. FFA: Jon Von Canon/Clay Frisbie 1991.

7   **Underdog (11 PG)** ★★★★ Overhanging offwidth leads to one bolt just past roof. After mounting roof, this leads to a left-facing dihedral crack with a fixed stopper (unless some paltry climber pilfered it). Continue up to an overhanging, flaring handcrack. This route is very sustained. It is just as overhung as it is tall. A large cam helps protect the five-inch crack at the start of the route. There is a very loose section of blocks on the right side of the wall about ten feet under the bolt. You might use caution before using them as holds. These babies are a timebomb just waiting to blow. A big block falling on top of your belayer's chest might just ruin you or your partner's perfectly good day. 65 feet. FFA: Clay Frisbie/Chuck Caughlin 11/93.

8   **Thick Passage (10)** ★★ Is offwidth climbing enjoyable? Yes! When you are done with it. An overhanging crack leads through a roof system and finishes with a flaring offwidth crack. 65 feet. FFA: Clay Frisbie/Tom Hancock 1991.

9   **Diamond in the Moss (11–)** ★★★ Striking left-facing thin dihedral crack. Climb fifteen feet to get started in the thin dihedral crack (5.11–) after which several 5.9 to 5.10 moves follow to render an excellent route. This would be a four-star route except that the start is prone to wetness. 60 feet. FFA: Clay Frisbie/Woody Delp 1991.

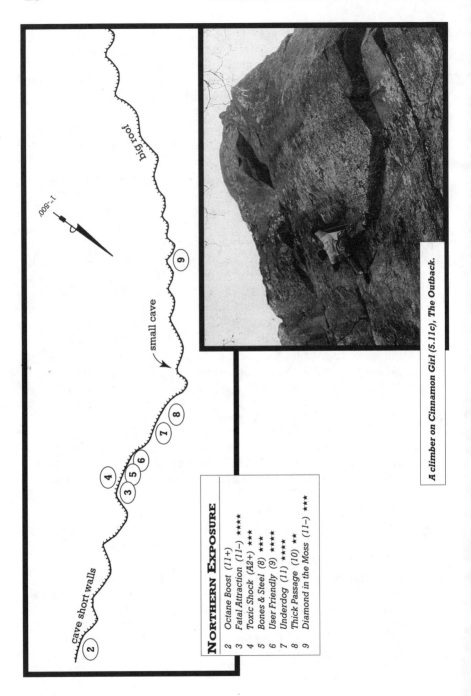

A climber on Cinnamon Girl (5.11c), The Outback.

NORTHERN EXPOSURE

2	Octane Boost (11+)
3	Fatal Attraction (11−) ★★★★
4	Toxic Shock (A2+) ★★★
5	Bones & Steel (8) ★★★
6	User Friendly (9) ★★★★
7	Underdog (11) ★★★★
8	Thick Passage (10) ★★
9	Diamond in the Moss (11−) ★★★

cave short walls

small cave

big roof

1" = 500'

THE OUTBACK

This area can be approached from a few ways, most of them taking ten to fifteen minutes. The Dog Walkdown, the trail that leads from the road, is the easiest approach. This area contains a very high concentration of routes varying from hard sport routes to moderate crack climbs. Good climbing can be found year round with trees for shade during the summer heat. In the winter the sun hits many of the faces in the afternoon. A wide conglomeration of routes transpiring at the 5.10 level on solid rock, makes this a popular destination for the aspiring weekend warrior.

10   **Frog Hair (9)** ★★★   Left-facing dihedral crack starts out as an offwidth crack and narrows to an enjoyable finger dihedral crack to distinguish the route as a 5.9 classic. As with many of the routes on this side of the bluff, moss and lichen are just part of the climbing experience. 65 feet. FFA: Clay Frisbie/Berry Rabe 1992.

11   **Cinnamon Girl (11c)** ★★★   Face climb up pockets left of the arête past three bolts and the crux (5.11c). At first horizontal crack (great rest spot) traverse left to continue climb up the face. This route is full of several 5.10 moves. One or two well defined tricky crux moves. Should be a four-star route but has received three stars because some may find the lichen and dirt on route not hygienic enough for a good sport route. Six bolts protect this sustained mixed route. Cams to protect horizontal cracks from one-inch to four-inches would be a very welcome item to have. Even though this route has a rap anchor, the climb is not complete until you can completely top out (5.11A)! Two-bolt anchor. 75 feet. FFA: Frisbie/Stites/Delp 5/94.

E OUTBACK

Frog Hair (9) ★★★
Cinnamon Girl (11c) ★★★
Left and Out (8+) ★
Euthanasia (13a) ★★★★
Want To Be Famous (8+) ★★★

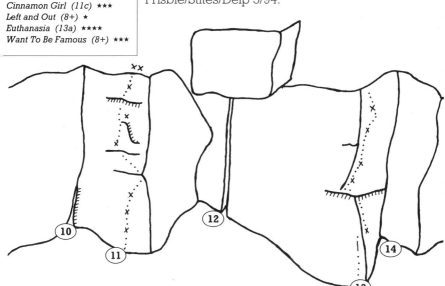

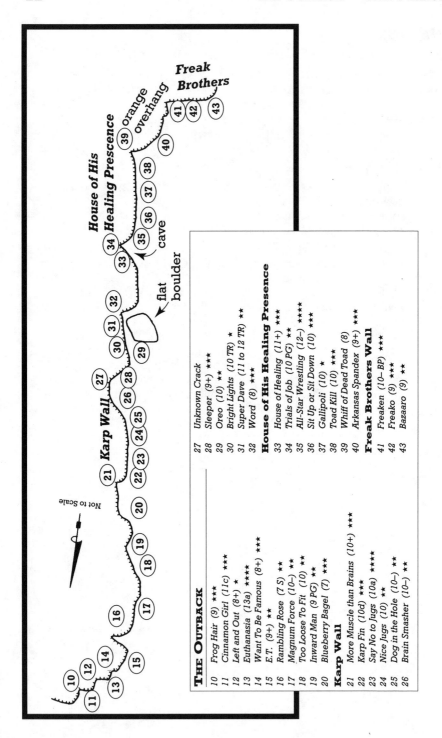

Not to Scale

House of His
Healing Prescence

Freak
Brothers

orange
overhang

cave

flat
boulder

Karp Wall

THE OUTBACK

10 Frog Hair (9) ★★★
11 Cinnamon Girl (11c) ★★★
12 Left and Out (8+) ★
13 Euthanasia (13a) ★★★★
14 Want To Be Famous (8+) ★★★
15 E.T. (9+) ★★
16 Rambling Rose (7 S) ★★
17 Magnum Force (10–) ★★
18 Too Loose To Fit (10) ★★
19 Inward Man (9 PG) ★★
20 Blueberry Bagel (7) ★★★

Karp Wall

21 More Muscle than Brains (10+) ★★★
22 Karp Fin (10d) ★★★
23 Say No to Jugs (10a) ★★★★
24 Nice Jugs (10) ★★
25 Dog in the Hole (10–) ★★
26 Brain Smasher (10–) ★★

27 Unknown Crack
28 Sleeper (9+) ★★★
29 Oreo (10) ★★
30 Bright Lights (10 TR) ★
31 Super Dave (11 to 12 TR) ★★
32 Word (8) ★★★

House of His Healing Presence

33 House of Healing (11+) ★★★
34 Trials of Job (10 PG) ★★
35 All-Star Wrestling (12–) ★★★★
36 Sit Up or Sit Down (10) ★★★
37 Gallipoli (10) ★
38 Toad Kill (10) ★★★
39 Whiff of Dead Toad (8)
40 Arkansas Spandex (9+) ★★★

Freak Brothers Wall

41 Freaken (10– BP) ★★★
42 Freako (9) ★★★
43 Bazaaro (9) ★★

12   **Left and Out (8+)** ★ Large dihedral crack system left to exit. 60 feet. FFA: Jon Von Canon/Berry Rabe 1992.

13   **Euthanasia (13a)** ★★★★ One of the more prominent arêtes at Sam's, it is difficult to miss this line if you walk by it. Begin on the low-angle arête (5.10) which leads to the pronounced, orange, jutting arête. This next part of the arête contains several sustained moves which await your enjoyment. Five bolts for protection. 60 feet. FFA: Clay Frisbie 1991.

14   **Want To Be Famous (8+)** ★★★ Left-facing dihedral crack just right of *Euthanasia*, loose rock. 60 feet. FFA: Woody Delp 1991.

15   **E.T. (9+)** ★★ Left-facing fist roof crack. Thirty feet of moderate face climbing lead to the fist crack. 50-55 feet. FFA: Clay Frisbie/Tom Hancock 1991.

16   **Rambling Rose (7 S)** ★★ Climb up face in the corridor going left and up the path of least resistance. 60 feet.

17   **Magnum Force (10–)** ★★ Eye-catching, left-arching roof crack. Also, on top above this wall, are some excellent boulders for bouldering and a phenomenal place to hang out and enjoy the view and relax. 50 feet. FFA: Jon Von Canon/Clay Frisbie 1991.

18   **Too Loose To Fit (10)** ★★ Start up 5.8 offwidth to an offwidth in the roof. Head butts and leg jams are a prerequisite for this climb. 55 feet. FFA: Clay Frisbie/Chuck Caughlin 10/93.

19   **Inward Man (9 PG)** ★★ On left side of protruding column, stem up large chimney (5.8) to a small overhanging handcrack. FFA: Clay Frisbie 10/93.

20   **Blueberry Bagel (7)** ★★★ On right side of protruding column is finger-and-hand-size crack in a small corner. 50 feet.

KARP WALL

This wall is adorned with several nice horns and jug holds that make excellent protection when properly looped, twenty-four-inch slings work great.

21   **More Muscle than Brains (10+)** ★★★ This short but sweet route is reminiscent of Red Rock Point roof climbing at its finest. To start the route, third class thirty feet to the base of the fifteen-foot, dead-horizontal roof with a fist-size crack. Move under the roof doing several 5.10 moves using the handrail located inside the crack and turn the lip with a pumpy 5.10+ move. 45 feet. FFA: Clay Frisbie/Woody Delp 1991.

22   **Karp Fin (10d)** ★★★ Arête with orange rock that looks like a dorsal fin. Face climb right side of arête past six bolts on sustained 5.10 face climbing. This is about as close to a clip-and-go route as you can get. To not alarm some unsuspecting sport

climber, there are no belay anchor bolts, but the mother lode of chickenheads located at the top of the prow makes an interesting belay point. A key hold broke changing this route from a 5.10 to 5.10d. 70 feet. FFA: Hancock/Frisbie/Hughes 5/94.

23   **Say No to Jugs (10a)** ★★★★   Five feet right of arête in a right-angling thin crack on orange face. Follow crack up forty feet of superb 5.8 climbing to first bolt. Continue up and right past two more bolts (5.10b). Even with three bolts, this route is more of an adventure classic because of the amount of protection it will accept and is needed. A high quality route well worth doing. 65 feet. FFA: Frisbie/Caughlin/Sosinavage 6/94.

24   **Nice Jugs (10)** ★★   Follow right-angling crack and veer left to a large sloped ledge in the middle of Karp Wall. Climb straight up past two bolts to blank section (5.10). Two made-to-order jugs to sling for protection after the crux. Continue up and veer right for same finish as *Dog in the Hole*. 65 feet. FFA: Frisbie/Caughlin/Sosinavage 6/94.

25   **Dog in the Hole (10–)** ★★   Follow right-angling crack. Continue up this crack to bolt. Then continue on above bolt on face straight up to large tree. Great stopper placements! 65 feet. FFA: Frisbie/Caughlin/Kevin Sosinavage 6/94.

26   **Brain Smasher (10–)** ★★   Corner just right of Karp Wall is right-arching crack. Start back inside offwidth up to a classic hand jam crack. Follow crack through right-arching roof. Although short, this is a superb crack climb. 30 feet.

27   **Unknown Crack**   Crack inside corner. 25 feet.

28   **Sleeper (9+)** ★★★   Blank twenty-foot face leads to an obvious crack system. Face climb bouldery start (5.9+) beginning just left under the right-facing dihedral crack. Climb flakes twenty feet then traverse into the crack. The pro is a little sketchy until gaining access to the crack system. Enjoyable 5.9 climbing with a surprising mix of protection all the way to the top. 65 feet. FFA: Clay Frisbie/Tom Hancock 6/94.

29   **Oreo (10)** ★★   A 5.8 chimney narrows down to an offwidth roof (5.10). 55 feet. FFA: Clay Frisbie/Tom Hancock 10/93.

30   **Bright Lights (10 TR)** ★   Face climb up middle of wall just left of left-angling crack. 55 feet.

31   **Super Dave (11 to 12 TR)** ★★   Left-angling, diagonal, thin crack, reach dependent. 55 feet.

32   **Word (8)** ★★★   A classic perfect handcrack on black rock. A short climb well worth doing.

HOUSE OF HIS HEALING PRESENCE

33 **House of Healing (11+)** ★★★ Boulder up to mount the orange arête. Climb past three bolts then step right across space into the crack system with the belay anchor. Top out on *Trials of Job* or lower at the anchor. 65 feet. FFA: Clay Frisbie/Chuck Caughlin 10/93.

34 **Trials of Job (10 PG)** ★★ Start in the back of the cave. Climb up crack behind flake (5.10–) up to the roof. Climb across the bomb bay chimney (5.8) to where the chimney stops and the crack narrows down. Step down and around the lip (5.10) to a great stance and a bolt. Continue in the right-angling crack system (5.9) to the top. Because the bomb bay chimney offers relatively little protection, this section is just as dangerous for the second as it is for the lead. 30 feet sideways, 65 feet up. FFA: Frisbie/Caughlin 10/93.

35 **All-Star Wrestling (12–)** ★★★★ On the right side of the mouth of the cave, start in the crack system that runs along a large looking flake. Ascend the crack into the overhanging offwidth (5.11+); turn the lip of the overhang (5.12–) onto a (5.9) face. To save on rope drag, set up belay in the middle of face fifteen feet above and to the right of the overhang. From this belay you can finish either crack system left or right (both 5.10) or brake down the belay traverse right and down with no protection (5.9). There is nothing like wrestling a good offwidth crack to lose some skin and get your blood flowing. This route may not be long, but it packs a powerful punch. Hopefully, you can pin this opponent before it pins you. 35 feet. FFA: Wilford/Frisbie/Stites 1991.

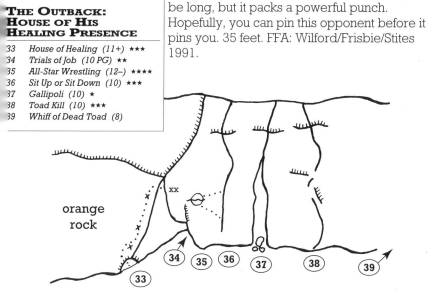

orange
rock

36   **Sit Up or Sit Down (10)** ★★★   Flaring crack leads to a left-facing short roof crack. Hard lieback to turn roof leads to jugs. 60 feet. FFA: Jon Von Canon 1991.

37   **Gallipoli (10)** ★   Chimney (5.8) leads to roof crack above. 55 feet.

38   **Toad Kill (10)** ★★★   This popular route is the obvious handcrack at the base of the route. Moderate crack leads to left-angling roof crack. Left-angling, hand/finger crack leads to jugs at top. 55 feet. FFA: Clay Frisbie/Tom Hancock 1991.

39   **Whiff of Dead Toad (8)**   Body size chimney with a handcrack in the back. 35 feet.

40   **Arkansas Spandex (9+)** ★★★   Large crack angling through two bulges. 55 feet. FFA: Jon Von Canon/Randy Schell 1991.

FREAK BROTHERS WALL

41   **Freaken (10– BP)** ★★★   First crack right of chimney walkdown. Climb crack up to the ledge. Then stem over to the chimney to get back down. Great boulder problem. 30 feet.

42   **Freako (9)** ★★★   Finger-hand crack system located in the middle of Freak Brothers Wall. This crack may look easy but it is surprisingly sustained. 40 feet. FFA: Woody Delp/Tom Hancock 1991.

43   **Bazaaro (9)** ★★   Slightly overhanging handcrack leads to a jug bash finish. 50 feet. FFA: Clay Frisbie/Tom Hancock 1991.

44   **Garden Salad (10–)**   Rotten orange face to a short roof with good pro followed by a short, flaring crack and runout slab. 60 feet. FFA: Stites 1991.

45   **Cave (7?)**   Cave crack?

SEED WALL

46   **Pooh Corner (6)** ★   A dihedral crack on a low-angle wall. Classic moderate route. 50 feet.

47   **Tempted & Tried (9 S)**   Straight up face right of *Pooh Corner*. FFA: Clay Frisbie 1991.

48   **Where's Tom? (7)** ★★★   Starts with large crack that narrows down to a large, left-facing flake. Continue in crack to the top. 50 feet. FFA: Dennis Nelms 1991.

49   **Grandaddy's Delight (7)** ★★★   Large crack. 50 feet.

50   **Burning Smear (10d TR)** ★★   Start on friction to right of thin seam. Follow seam until horizontal, then left over little bulging roof to top. 55 feet.

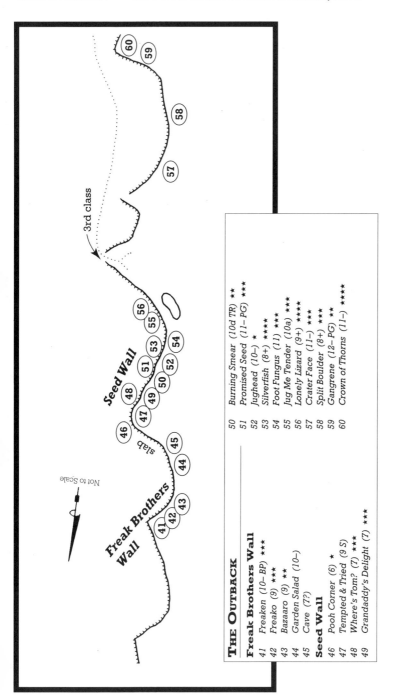

3rd class

Seed Wall

slab

Freak Brothers
Wall

Not to Scale

THE OUTBACK

Freak Brothers Wall

41   Freaken (10– BP) ★★★
42   Freako (9) ★★★
43   Bazaaro (9) ★★
44   Garden Salad (10–)
45   Cave (7?)

Seed Wall

46   Pooh Corner (6) ★
47   Tempted & Tried (9 S)
48   Where's Tom? (7) ★★★
49   Grandaddy's Delight (7) ★★★
50   Burning Smear (10d TR) ★★
51   Promised Seed (11– PG) ★★★
52   Jughead (10–) ★
53   Silverfish (8+) ★★★★
54   Foot Fungus (11) ★★★
55   Jug Me Tender (10a) ★★★
56   Lonely Lizard (9+) ★★★★
57   Crater Face (11–) ★★★
58   Split Boulder (8+) ★★★
59   Gangrene (12– PG) ★★
60   Crown of Thorns (11–) ★★★★

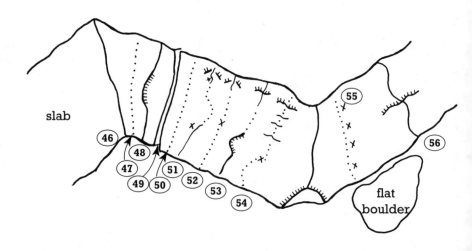

51   Promised Seed (11– PG) ★★★   Boulder up to where the thin crack system begins. Where the crack stops, continue up (5.11–) on less than positive holds, then traverse left to the thin dihedral crack to top out (5.10). Two fixed pins, if they have not been stolen again. Protection: A little runout above the first fixed piton. 55 feet. FFA: Clay Frisbie/Woody Delp 6/91.

52   Jughead (10–) ★   Ten feet left of *Silverfish*, ascend jugs to a bolt, then up and left through roof. 55 feet. FFA: Tom Karpowiz/Mike Davidson 1992.

53   Silverfish (8+) ★★★★   Climb crack twenty feet to small left-facing roof. After roof, angle right to turn next small roof with a crack. 55 feet. FFA: Woody Delp 6/91.

54   Foot Fungus (11) ★★★   One-bolt face climb that ascends waterstreak that has a small roof to top out. Protection: Small tri-cams work wonders. 55 feet. FFA: Mike Stites 1991.

55   Jug Me Tender (10a) ★★★   Start off boulder and jug bash up orange face left of *Lonely Lizard*. Four bolts adequately protect sustained climbing on this clip-and-go route. 60 feet. FFA: Sean Burns/Amy Calvert 5/94.

56 **Lonely Lizard (9+)** ★★★★ Located just downhill from the second walkdown. Obvious line with a hand-to-finger crack located on orange, slightly overhanging rock. May be tricky to protect. 60 feet. FFA: Clay Frisbie/Woody Delp 1991.

57 **Crater Face (11–)** ★★★ Located one hundred feet right of second walkdown. Orange face covered with finger pockets; three bolts on left side of an arête. This route looks like a good candidate for finger tendinitis but the holds are better than they look. Miss the second clip and you will crater. 60 feet. FFA: Mike Stites/Mike Davidson 1991.

58 **Split Boulder (8+)** ★★★ The slab with the noticeable split boulder that abides atop. Meander up slab (5.6) angling right to a bolt at a slight overhang. After mounting the vertical section (5.8), continue up with moderate climbing to the split boulder handcrack that looms overhead (5.8+). This is an excellent mellow route with some 5.6 runout. FFA: Frisbie/Caughlin/Sosinavage 6/94.

59 **Gangrene (12– PG)** ★★ Thin crack in the shallow dihedral just left of *Crown of Thorns*. Several crux, boulder stemming moves lead up to the lip of the dihedral roof. At the lip, tricky protection can be had to protect turning the lip. The best protection is having a good spotter (hopefully a really big guy with strong arms). This route does collect dirt in the cracks. It might be best to rap down to clean out the crack before leading it or you may be in for an unpleasant surprise. FFA: Frisbie/Stites/Nelms (great spotter) 1992.

60 **Crown of Thorns (11–)** ★★★★ Handcrack coming out of a small cave (5.11–). The climbing above the roof is 5.8 with a couple of tricky moves near the top. This route may not look like much, but it is actually an excellent upside-down roof handcrack , a great warm up for Arkansas Reality that can be well protected. 50 feet. FFA: Woody Delp/Eric Peterson 1991.

DOWN UNDER WALL

61 **Want to be a Man (10+ PG)** ★★ Leftmost crack on Down Under Wall. Face climb fifteen feet up to a gentle sloping crack on orange rock (5.10)—it's more difficult than it appears. After crack ends traverse left to a right-facing, overhanging dihedral crack. Strenuous liebacks and handjams lead to the top. 50 feet. FFA: Clay Frisbie/Woody Delp 1991.

62 **Yin and Yang (12a)** ★★★ This is the center roof crack on Down Under Wall. Face climb steep face leaping from one large jug to another (5.10) to the base of the roof. At the roof, strain to achieve

loose handjams; then move up to a more secure handjam to turn the roof (5.12a). Five bolts (stoppers and cams might come in handy). This is a superb warmup for *Ultimate Frisbee*. 65 feet. FFA: Frisbie/Caughlin/Delp 6/94.

63   **Walk About (9)** ★★★   Three separate cracks lead to the base of the short, left-facing, dihedral crack. The middle crack is the hardest (5.9). At the dihedral, pull up and over (5.9). Continue up and to the left. This is definitely an adventure climb. 50 feet. FFA: Clay Frisbie/Woody Delp 6/91.

64   **Feline Grace (11– PG)** ★★   Overhanging grey face just left of arête. Start by stemming up face with thin crack, then left up face past a bolt (5.11–), then back right toward arête up to the second bolt. From roof go straight up on jugs. Very sustained and dynamic! 60 feet. FFA: Tom Hancock/Clay Frisbie 5/94.

65   **Spank Me (10d)** ★★★★   Obvious orange arête lined with large jug holds on the left and featureless on the right. Five bolts on the right side of arête protect this popular route which is predominately climbed on the left side. A two-bolt anchor at the top on the right side. 65 feet. FFA: Gary Olsen 5/94.

66   **Me Belly Be Full (7)**   Large chimney dihedral. Climb inside of chimney. This is one of the easiest ways to get to the top in this vicinity. 55 feet. FFA: Mike Stites 1991.

67   **Outback Traverse (10+ BP)** ★★★★   Striking horizontal crack that begins six feet off ground on the left side of the arête. The traverse starts right of *Sonic Love Jugs* and follows the horizontal crack for about eighty feet till the crack completely ends just at *Pentecost*. 75 feet.

68   **Sonic Love Jugs (11+)** ★★★★   A few feet left of arête, start up face that has two bolts and several horizontal cracks that accept a wide range of protection. Numerous sustained 5.10 moves lead to the last bolt near the top for one superb crux before topping out. 65 feet. FFA: Clay Frisbie/ Woody Delp 1991.

69   **Cling to Evil (12b)** ★★★   A sporty sport climb on the right side of the arête. Climb along arête past four bolts. Face climb is extremely sustained and technical, a prized red point! This route might be height dependent because the rating seems to vary widely from 5.11d to 5.12d. Of course, I may be a bit biased because *Cling to Evil* is an appropriate name for my experience with this classic finger-tweaking route. 65 feet. FFA: Hancock/Gilbert/Stites/Frisbie 1993.

70a   **Pork Soda (10d)** ★★   Ascend past one bolt and one fixed pin on this mixed route. 65 feet. FFA: Sean Burns.

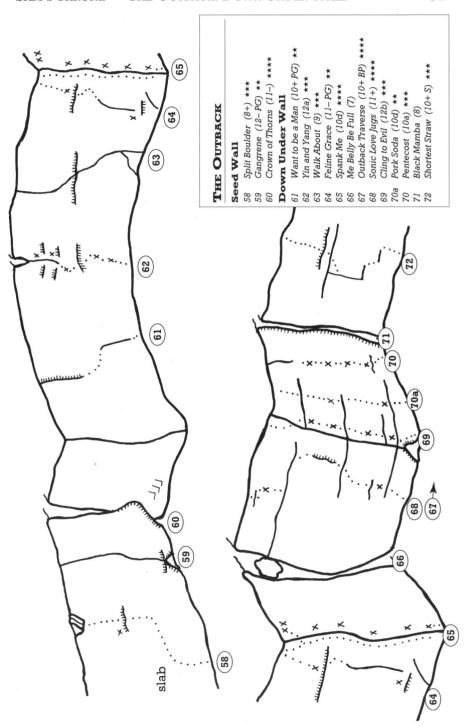

THE OUTBACK

Seed Wall

58 Split Boulder (8+) ★★★
59 Gangrene (12– PG) ★★
60 Crown of Thorns (11–) ★★★★

Down Under Wall

61 Want to be a Man (10+ PG) ★★
62 Yin and Yang (12a) ★★★
63 Walk About (9) ★★★
64 Feline Grace (11– PG) ★★
65 Spank Me (10d) ★★★★
66 Me Belly Be Full (7)
67 Outback Traverse (10+ BP) ★★★★
68 Sonic Love Jugs (11+) ★★★★
69 Cling to Evil (12b) ★★★
70a Pork Soda (10d) ★★
70 Pentecost (10a) ★★★
71 Black Mamba (8)
72 Shortest Straw (10+ S) ★★★

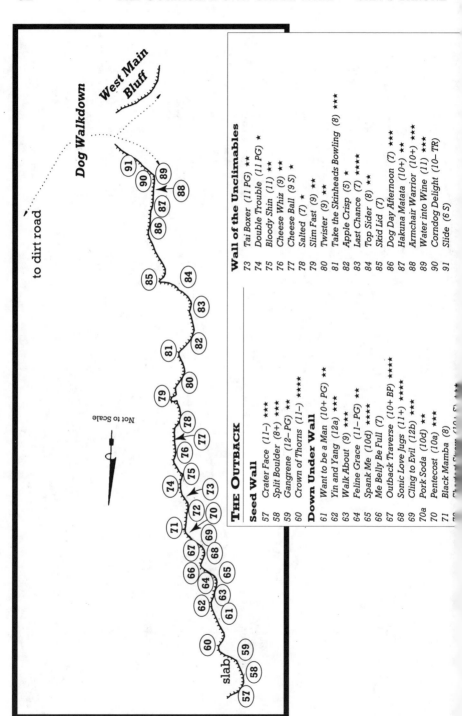

to dirt road

Dog Walkdown

West Main Bluff

Not to Scale

slab

THE OUTBACK

Seed Wall

57   Crater Face (11–) ★★★
58   Split Boulder (8+) ★★★
59   Gangrene (12– PG) ★★
60   Crown of Thorns (11–) ★★★★

Down Under Wall

61   Want to be a Man (10+ PG) ★★
62   Yin and Yang (12a) ★★★
63   Walk About (9) ★★★
64   Feline Grace (11– PG) ★★
65   Spank Me (10d) ★★★★
66   Me Belly Be Full (7)
67   Outback Traverse (10+ BP) ★★★★
68   Sonic Love Jugs (11+) ★★★★
69   Cling to Evil (12b) ★★★
70a   Pork Soda (10d) ★★
70   Pentecost (10a) ★★★
71   Black Mamba (8)

Wall of the Unclimbables

73   Tai Boxer (11 PG) ★★
74   Double Trouble (11 PG) ★
75   Bloody Shin (11) ★★
76   Cheese Whiz (9) ★★
77   Cheese Ball (9 S) ★
78   Salted (7) ★
79   Slim Fast (9) ★★
80   Twister (9) ★★
81   Take the Skinheads Bowling (8) ★★★
82   Apple Crisp (5) ★
83   Last Chance (7) ★★★★
84   Top Sider (8) ★★
85   Skid Lid (7)
86   Dog Day Afternoon (7) ★★★
87   Hakuna Matata (10+) ★★
88   Armchair Warrior (10+) ★★★
89   Water into Wine (11) ★★★
90   Corndog Delight (10– TR)
91   Slide (6 S)

70 **Pentecost (10a)** ★★★ Ascend middle of face past four bolts. Small cams and stoppers helpful for the top out. 55 feet. FFA: Clay Frisbie/Chuck Caughlin 6/94.

71 **Black Mamba (8)** Start in offwidth in black rock that reduces to finger-and-hand crack. This route is typically wet. 60 feet.

72 **Shortest Straw (10+ S)** ★★★ Thirty feet right of the black dihedral is a thin crack system. Boulder up (5.10+) and left past horizontal cracks to where the thin crack begins. Several sustained 5.10 moves lead to the roof (protection may be good but very physical to place). Large cams under the roof and a calm head are the best protection for the runout above (5.9). Routes like this make lead climbing exciting and memorable. This route was top-roped once before it was led. 60 feet. FFA: Frisbie/Hancock/Delp/Stites 10/92.

WALL OF THE UNCLIMBABLES

73 **Tai Boxer (11 PG)** ★★ Same start as *Bloody Shin* then traverse across face to the roof crack on the left. Sustained climbing through overhanging handcrack (5.11). Continue up and right. 60 feet. FFA: Clay Frisbie/Bill Hughes 5/94.

74 **Double Trouble (11 PG)** ★ Ascend to overhanging roof with hand-and-fist crack (5.10). After overcoming roof, move left to a thin, flaring crack and top out (5.11). 60 feet. FFA: Clay Frisbie/Tom Hancock 5/92.

75 **Bloody Shin (11)** ★★ Ascend fistcrack that goes up and moves right to base of roof with fingercrack. Bolt located halfway out roof. Turn roof (5.11) continue up and right. 60 feet. FFA: Clay Frisbie/Bill Hughes 5/94.

76 **Cheese Whiz (9)** ★★ Take left obvious thin crack up a large sloping ledge halfway up the wall to another thin crack. Continue to top. 45 feet. FFA: Woody Delp/Tom Hancock 4/93.

77 **Cheese Ball (9 S)** ★ Take right obvious thin crack up a large sloping ledge halfway up the wall to another thin crack. Continue to top. 45 feet. FFA: Tom Hancock/Woody Delp 4/93.

78 **Salted (7)** ★ Left-facing hand-and-fist crack. 40 feet.

79 **Slim Fast (9)** ★★ Obvious body-size chimney crack in right-facing dihedral. Corn fed boys might find this chimney a tight squeeze. After twenty-five feet the chimney narrows down to a finger-and-hand crack. Good luck on finding this one dry! If it is dry, do it and find out what a squeeze chimney truly is. This ain't no pretty boy's climb! 45 feet. FFA: Woody Delp/Tom Hancock 4/93.

80   **Twister (9)** ★★   Left-facing dihedral handcrack winding through two overhanging bulges. It is easiest to start a few feet to the right instead of the watergroove that is directly in line with the route. 45 feet. FFA: Tom Hancock/Woody Delp 4/93.

81   **Take the Skinheads Bowling (8)** ★★★   A black, flaring, winding water groove crack makes for an interesting and enjoyable route. 45 feet. FFA: Clay Frisbie/Woody Delp 5/94.

82   **Apple Crisp (5)** ★   Chimney up slab. 30 feet.

83   **Last Chance (7)** ★★★★   Quality line up left-facing dihedral handcrack that is lined with good handholds. This is a popular route to lead with generous climbing and protection. 50 feet.

84   **Top Sider (8)** ★★   Left-angling, overhanging fist crack. 40 feet.

85   **Skid Lid (7)**   Climb inside chimney. 40 feet.

86   **Dog Day Afternoon (7)** ★★★   Classic right-angling dihedral crack. A variety of moves and sustained climbing make this an excellent route. 50 feet.

87   **Hakuna Matata (10+)** ★★   Left of *Armchair Warrior*, follow crack (5.8) to base of roof. Traverse left to bolt and the next crack system. Mixed route two bolts. 60 feet. FFA: Frisbie/Caughlan/Von Canon 3/96.

88   **Armchair Warrior (10+)** ★★★   First crack around from Dog Walkdown. Climb thirty feet up orange face (5.9 PG) to the base of where the prominent roof crack begins. One bolt located just under roof; shares two-bolt anchor with *Water into Wine*. 60 feet. FFA: Clay Frisbie/Chuck Caughlan 10/93.

89   **Water into Wine (11)** ★★★   Orange overhanging face just right of *Armchair Warrior*, top out in groove to the left. Mixed route, two-inch to half-inch gear, plus five bolts, two-bolt anchor. 60 feet. FFA: Frisbie/Caughlan/Von Canon 3/96.

90   **Corndog Delight (10– TR)**   Forty feet left of Dog Walkdown, climb up a mossy crack for ten feet to chickenheads at top. Turn roof on good jug. Then climb the slab/face straight up. 40 feet.

91   **Slide (6 S)**   Ascend slab left of walkdown. 30 feet.

Tom Hancock on Sonic Love Jugs (5.11+) ★★★★, The Outback, Down Under Wall. Photo: Woody Delp.

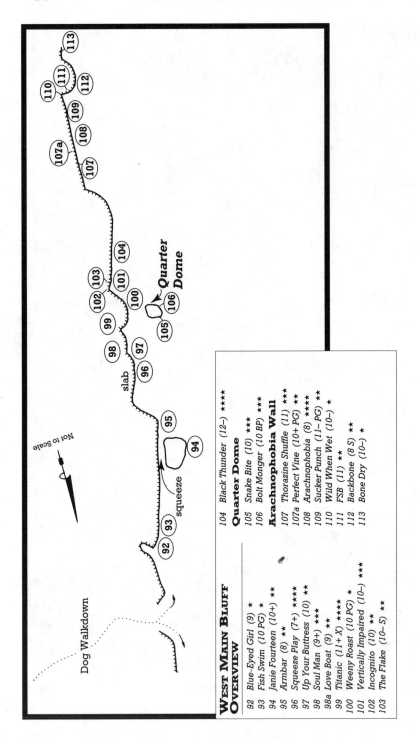

WEST MAIN BLUFF OVERVIEW

92 Blue-Eyed Girl (9) *
93 Fish Swim (10 PG) *
94 Janie Fourteen (10+) **
95 Armbar (8) **
96 Squeeze Play (7+) ****
97 Up Your Buttress (10) **
98 Soul Man (9+) ***
98a Love Boat (9) **
99 Titanic (11+ X) ****
100 Weeny Roast (10 PG) *
101 Vertically Impaired (10–) ***
102 Incognito (10) **
103 The Flake (10–5) **

104 Black Thunder (12–) ****

Quarter Dome

105 Snake Bite (10) ***
106 Bolt Monger (10 BP) ***

Arachnophobia Wall

107 Thorazine Shuffle (11) ***
107a Perfect Vine (10+ PG) ***
108 Arachnophobia (8) ****
109 Sucker Punch (11– PG) **
110 Wild When Wet (10–) *
111 FSB (11) **
112 Backbone (8 S) **
113 Bone Dry (10–) *

WEST MAIN BLUFF

The West Bluff is a ten- to fifteen-minute approach via the Dog Walkdown or The Ramp. Most of the routes in this area are well shaded with climbing best during summer and fall. Several of the developed routes are slightly dirty but well worth climbing, offering some excellent adventure routes. During the winter, on rare occasions, several phenomenal ice climbs form along this part of the bluff for brief period of time.

92 **Blue-Eyed Girl (9)** ★ Boulder up ten feet through overhang up to a flaring offwidth. 35 feet.

93 **Fish Swim (10 PG)** ★ Twenty feet right of *Blue-Eyed Girl*. A crack leads up ten feet to a flaring offwidth. 35 feet.

94 **Janie Fourteen (10+)** ★★ Located in the middle of the wall on the west side of the squeeze block. Climb straight up past two bolts (5.10+) through first bulge. At ledge traverse right to the roof crack (5.10). Two-bolt anchor. 65 feet. FFA: Frisbie/Schooler/Duncan 7/96.

95 **Armbar (8)** ★★ Short offwidth. 35 feet.

96 **Squeeze Play (7+)** ★★★★ Pronounced left-arching offwidth chimney crack, sustained matchless offwidth climbing! 60 feet. FFA: Barry Gilbert 1992.

97 **Up Your Buttress (10)** ★★ Handcrack cuts through a short roof just right of arête. 50 feet. FFA: Chuck Foster 1989.

98 **Soul Man (9+)** ★★★ Right-facing watergroove dihedral with thin crack. Lowe Balls and small stoppers could be a beneficial item to take up. FFA: Clay Frisbie/Woody Delp 9/91.

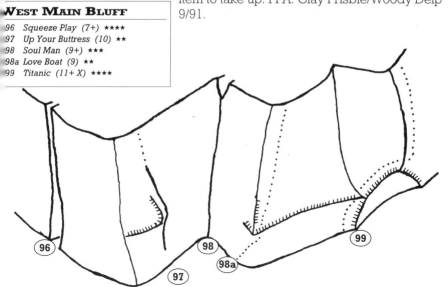

WEST MAIN BLUFF

96 *Squeeze Play (7+)* ★★★★
97 *Up Your Buttress (10)* ★★
98 *Soul Man (9+)* ★★★
98a *Love Boat (9)* ★★
99 *Titanic (11+ X)* ★★★★

98a **Love Boat (9)** ★★   Face climb over overhanging arête.

99   **Titanic (11+ X)** ★★★★   This beautiful face offers some great climbing on superb rock. This route ascends the north pronounced dished-out face and jutting arête. Climb up thirty feet through overhang (5.9) to the base of the face to the dished-out area. From the dished out area traverse up and right with some balancey technical moves (5.11) to the arête. Extremely exposed with a potentially bad pendulum fall at the crux. Continue with sustained pumpy climbing on the arête (5.10) to the top. This route may not be a classic lead but it is certainly a classic top-rope. This route was top-roped once before it was originally lead. 80 feet. FFA: Mark Wilford/Stites/Frisbie 4/91.

100 **Weeny Roast (10 PG)** ★   Orange arête face with jugs. Near top do direct finish (5.10 VS) and experience a real weeny roast or traverse right for same finish as *Vertically Impaired*. 70 feet. FFA: Clay Frisbie/Tom Hancock 1992.

101 **Vertically Impaired (10–)** ★★★   Low-angle wall; middle of face left of *Incognito* with two bolts. Finish on headwall. Some tri-cams or small cams might come in handy to finish on the headwall, two-bolt anchor. 60 feet. FFA: Frisbie/Schooler/Duncan 7/96.

102 **Incognito (10)** ★★   Ramp fifty feet left of *Black Thunder*. Crescent-moon-shaped thin dihedral crack on orange gently sloping face. This is a good place to find out if those little bitty stoppers and RPs really do work in sandstone. 55 feet. FFA: Woody Delp/Clay Frisbie 9/91.

103 **The Flake (10–S)** ★★   Flake left of *Incognito*, then continue on face. 50 feet. FFA: Clay Frisbie/Tom Hancock 10/91.

104 **Black Thunder (12–)** ★★★★   Smooth black face with three bolts. Start up the thin crack system and traverse right above the roof. After traverse, continue straight up past two bolts with sustained technical balance moves on less than positive holds (5.12–), a scarce commodity for climbing routes in this area. Three bolts with two-bolt anchor. 75 feet. FFA: Frisbie/Delp/Hancock 9/91.

QUARTER DOME

Quarter Dome is the thirty-foot boulder that is thirty yards downhill from Black Thunder.

105 **Snake Bite (10)** ★★★   Located on the northwest arête of Quarter Dome boulder, ascend straight up arête via a thin crack that starts midway up the right side past one fixed pin. This route is short and sweet. 35 feet. FFA: Frisbie/Hancock 1992.

ARACHNOPHOBIA WALL

106   Bolt Monger (10 BP) ★★★   On west side of Quarter Dome boulder, zigzag up right-facing flake. 25 feet.

107   Thorazine Shuffle (11) ★★★   The most obvious feature on this route is the overhang split by a fistcrack. Start up sloping crack thirty feet to where the first roof begins. A couple of moves (5.10) lead to a seven-foot roof with a fist size crack. Squeeze, grunt and thrash through the offwidth to overcome the roof (5.11) and continue fifty feet with moderate climbing to top. The best protection for this route is a long-sleeve shirt and a #4 Camalot. 80 feet. FFA: Clay Frisbie/Tom Hancock 1991.

107a   Perfect Vine (10+ PG) ★★   Just right of *Thorazine Shuffle* climb up face with horizontal cracks for protection. FFA: Bob Sheier/Tom Hancock 1996.

108   Arachnophobia (8) ★★★★   Obvious left-facing, outward-curving, fist-size dihedral crack system. A slab at the bottom leads to the start of the crack. Spectacular stances with sustained adventuresome climbing up this well defined route make this a classic. FFA: Woody Delp/Clay Frisbie 1991.

109   Sucker Punch (11– PG) ★★   Twenty feet up grey slab to a bolt. Traverse up and left following angling dike to a headwall with a thin crack. Turn small bulge (5.11–), a couple of hard moves lead to large jug holds to blast to the top. 60 feet. FFA: Woody Delp/Clay Frisbie 5/94.

110   Wild When Wet (10–) ★   Left-facing dihedral. Low-angle slab at the start of the route leads to the crack. Climb up route via crack until jugs on the left face can be reached.

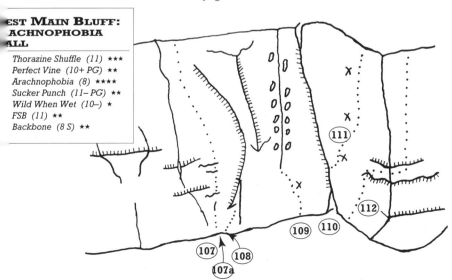

EST MAIN BLUFF:
ACHNOPHOBIA
ALL

Thorazine Shuffle (11) ★★★
Perfect Vine (10+ PG) ★★
Arachnophobia (8) ★★★★
Sucker Punch (11– PG) ★★
Wild When Wet (10–) ★
FSB (11) ★★
Backbone (8 S) ★★

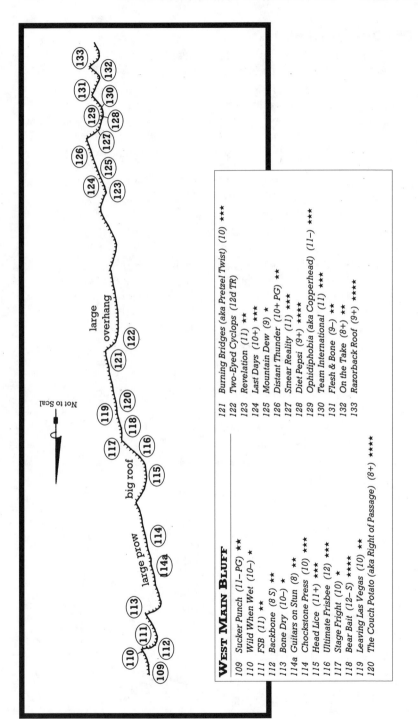

Not to Scale

large overhang

big roof

large prow

WEST MAIN BLUFF

109 Sucker Punch (11–PG) ★★
110 Wild When Wet (10–) ★
111 FSB (11) ★★
112 Backbone (8 S) ★★
113 Bone Dry (10–) ★
114a Guitars on Stun (8) ★★
114 Chockstone Press (10) ★★★
115 Head Lice (11+) ★★★
116 Ultimate Frisbee (12) ★★★
117 Stage Fright (10) ★
118 Bear Bait (12–S) ★★★★
119 Leaving Las Vegas (10) ★★
120 The Couch Potato (aka Right of Passage) (8+) ★★★★
121 Burning Bridges (aka Pretzel Twist) (10) ★★★
122 Two-Eyed Cyclops (12d TR)
123 Revelation (11) ★★
124 Last Days (10+) ★★★
125 Mountain Dew (9) ★
126 Distant Thunder (10+ PG) ★★
127 Smear Reality (11) ★★★
128 Diet Pepsi (9+) ★★★★
129 Ophidiphobia (aka Copperhead) (11–) ★★★
130 Team International (11) ★★★
131 Flesh & Bone (9–) ★★
132 On the Take (8+) ★★
133 Razorback Roof (9+) ★★★★

Climb to the top on huge handholds. Second version makes for a good sustained crack climb but a bit contrived: climb the route not using any of the jug handholds on the left face. Superb route for stemming. 65 feet. FFA: Clay Frisbie/Chuck Caughlin 3/94.

111   **FSB (11)** ★★   White slab with three bolts. Start *Wild When Wet* to the first bolt and traverse right (5.11). The best place to traverse seems to be with hands above and feet below first bolt. Then continue up past two more bolts (5.10–) to the top. 70 feet. FFA: Clay Frisbie/Woody Delp 5/94.

112   **Backbone (8 S)** ★★   Start a little to the right of *FSB* then traverse right under an overhang around arête that looks like a backbone. Ascend middle of a twenty-foot face that is lined with jug holds. 70 feet. FFA: Clay Frisbie/Woody Delp 5/94.

113   **Bone Dry (10–)** ★   Rarely bone dry watergroove slab leads to left-facing dihedral offwidth that is usually wet. Above offwidth roof the left face of dihedral is lined with jug holds. 80 feet. FFA: Clay Frisbie/Woody Delp 5/94.

114a   **Guitars on Stun (8)** ★★   This route is located under the conspicuous rectangular roof or prow that looms at the top of the route. Follow crack, at bottom pull roof using horns and knobs. Follow the corner along the left side of the large prow. This is an exciting route that is much easier than would first appear. 75 feet. FFA: Sandy Fleming/Scott Hall 1985.

114   **Chockstone Press (10)** ★★★   Located on the right side of the large overhanging prow is a crack system that runs through a large chimney with two different chockstones stuck in it near the top of the route. Start with the thin crack (5.10–) up to the squeeze chimney. At the overhanging chimney, squeeze (5.10) through at the first chockstone. This route is notorious for being wet. FFA: Clay Frisbie/Mike Baban 1996.

THE DARK SIDE WALL

115   **Head Lice (11+)** ★★★   Located in the middle of the massive overhang. Follow five bolts up orange face (5.10+) to offwidth roof above (5.11+). Mixed route, six bolts, two-bolt anchor. 75 feet. FFA: Clay Frisbie/Chandler Schooler 8/96.

116   **Ultimate Frisbee (12)** ★★★   Located on the right end of the massive overhang. Climb the green face twenty feet up to a fingercrack to go through the first roof (5.10) up to a ledge, the overhung handcrack looms above. Technical jams and unconventional body contortions lead past two bolts (5.12) and the offwidth above (5.11–) for a memorable experience. Being prone to wetness this route is best to climb from July to October

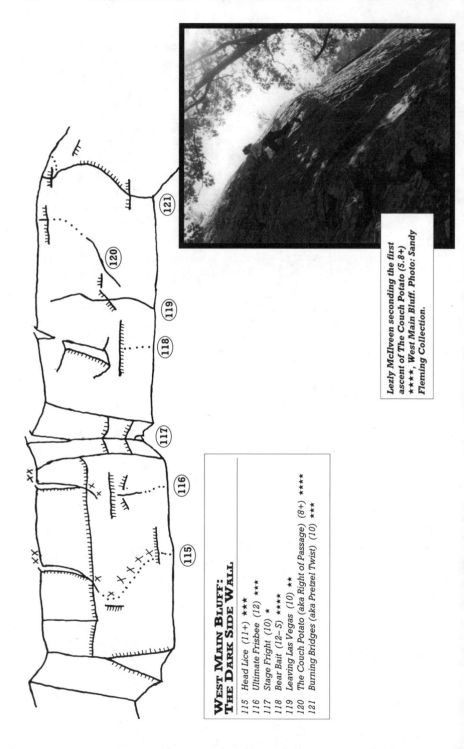

Lezly McIlveen seconding the first ascent of The Couch Potato (5.8+) ★★★★, West Main Bluff. Photo: Sandy Fleming Collection.

WEST MAIN BLUFF: THE DARK SIDE WALL

115   Head Lice (11+) ★★★
116   Ultimate Frisbee (12) ★★★
117   Stage Fright (10) ★
118   Bear Bait (12–S) ★★★★
119   Leaving Las Vegas (10) ★★
120   The Couch Potato (aka Right of Passage) (8+) ★★★★
121   Burning Bridges (aka Pretzel Twist) (10) ★★★

before the fall rain sets in. Best protection is tape and long pants. Two bolts. 75 feet. FFA: Clay Frisbie/Chandler Schooler 8/96.

117   **Stage Fright (10)** ★ Dirty, water drainage crack system that cuts through roof located at the right end of the massive overhang. This crack is rarely dry but provides some interesting moves and good protection pulling through the roof. 50 feet. FFA: Mike Stites/Mark Wilford 1992.

118   **Bear Bait (12– S)** ★★★★ Moderate climbing up thin crack leads to a conspicuous slightly overhanging right-facing thin dihedral crack. This route may be short but it is powerpacked (or should I say powerdraining). Launching into the overhang is committing on lead but a Lowe ball or Slider might bring some solace from crashing into the ledge below. 50 feet. [The first ascent of this route was three years in the making. This striking line on the first two attempts proved to be a harder and more committing lead than it originally appeared. To top-rope such a promising project would ruin the nature of what this route had to offer. A year-and-a-half later and few sleepless nights, I decided it was worth another try, again fear or common sense (sometimes a fine line) won out deciding to back out of the climb. Funny how time can wash away bad memories. Another year passed with another attempt ending with the grip of fear. This time Mark Wilford was along to take up the challenge. A two-rope belay on marginal protection with the only sound to break the silence a quivering "watch me," and a quick punch to the top mark the first ascent.] FFA: Mark Wilford/Clay Frisbie 1992.

119   **Leaving Las Vegas (10)** ★★ Left-angling crack system through short roof left of *The Couch Potato*. Same start as *The Couch Potato* but follow crack straight up through roof for some well-protected interesting climbing. FFA: Clay Frisbie/Chandler Schooler 8/96.

120   **The Couch Potato (aka Right of Passage) (8+)** ★★★★ Boulder up twenty feet to a distinct right-angling handcrack that can be seen from *Bear Bait*. Follow crack until it ends then continue straight up and right to large block with a horizontal crack (be careful of a loose block the size of a Volkswagen). Face climb to top out. This is a varied classic route of high quality at a moderate level. Length 100 feet (of course 30 feet of that is horizontal). FFA: Sandy Fleming/Lezley McIlveen/Scott Hall 1985.

121   **Burning Bridges (aka Pretzel Twist) (10)** ★★★ Prominent, outward-curving, thin left-facing dihedral crack with a watergroove at the base. This climb may look harder than it is, but the edges are good and the crack opens up just when protection looks improbable. This is an unique experience in

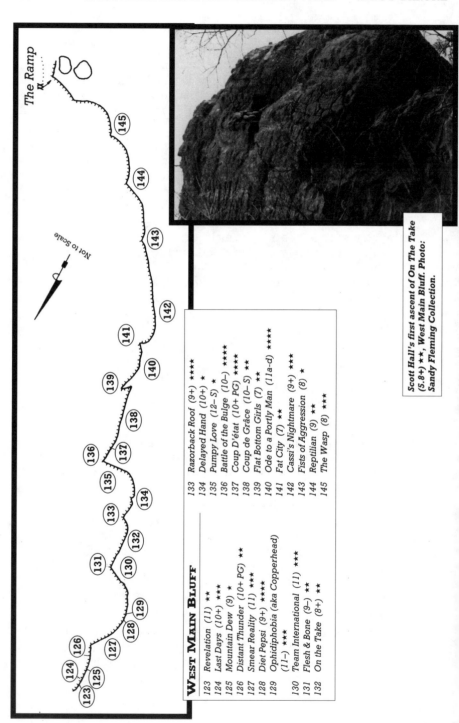

The Ramp

Not to Scale

WEST MAIN BLUFF

123 Revelation (11) ★★
124 Last Days (10+) ★★★
125 Mountain Dew (9) ★
126 Distant Thunder (10+ PG) ★★
127 Smear Reality (11) ★★★
128 Diet Pepsi (9+) ★★★★
129 Ophidiphobia (aka Copperhead) (11–) ★★★
130 Team International (11) ★★★
131 Flesh & Bone (9–) ★★
132 On the Take (8+) ★★

133 Razorback Roof (9+) ★★★★
134 Delayed Hand (10+) ★
135 Pumpy Love (12– S) ★
136 Battle of the Bulge (10–) ★★★★
137 Coup D'état (10+ PG) ★★★★
138 Coup de Grâce (10– S) ★★
139 Flat Bottom Girls (7) ★★
140 Ode to a Portly Man (11a-d) ★★★★
141 Fat City (7) ★★
142 Cassi's Nightmare (9+) ★★★
143 Fists of Aggression (8) ★
144 Reptilian (9) ★★
145 The Wasp (8) ★★★

Scott Hall's first ascent of On The Take (5.8+) ★★, West Main Bluff. Photo: Sandy Fleming Collection.

stemming and opposition technique. 70 feet. FFA: Sandy Fleming/Mark Lemons/John Gore 1985.

122   **Two-Eyed Cyclops (12d TR)**   Overhang right of *Burning Bridges*. Climb straight out overhang past two huecos then pull overhang (5.12d) on thin holds. 65 feet.

123   **Revelation (11)** ★★   Rotten, thirty-foot, curving crack (5.9) leads to a fingercrack that bisects a ten-foot roof. A bolt halfway out the roof protects the crux move. Jugs above make for moderate climbing. A long sling ready to loop a horn might help ease the nerves when turning the roof. 75 feet. FFA: Clay Frisbie/Chuck Caughlin 1/94.

124   **Last Days (10+)** ★★★   Climb fifteen feet up to an overhanging finger-and-hand crack. One bolt protects turning roof and wiggling into the flaring offwidth (5.10+). Continue sustained (5.8) climbing in flaring offwidth. 75 feet. FFA: Clay Frisbie/Chuck Caughlin 1/94.

125   **Mountain Dew (9)** ★   Start in large sickle shaped right-facing crack (5.8). Climb crack thirty-five feet, finish climb on lichen-covered knobs and chickenheads (5.9) to the top. 60 feet.

126   **Distant Thunder (10+ PG)** ★★   Face climb just right of *Mountain Dew*. Climb face through two thin crack systems moving left up face. Route intersects *Mountain Dew* at the top of the sickle-shaped crack then continues straight up. 60 feet. FFA: Clay Frisbie/Tom Hancock 1991.

127   **Smear Reality (11)** ★★★   Vertical friction slab. Traverse right from corner to middle of wall and then straight up face to crack system above. Less than positive holds devise a technically difficult route that requires the use of good balance (a unique route for Sam's Throne). Mixed route with three bolts, two-bolt anchor. 65 feet. FFA: Frisbie/Duncan 7/96.

128   **Diet Pepsi (9+)** ★★★★   The most obvious feature on this route is the well-defined, twenty-foot, four- to five-inch dihedral crack located in the middle of the route. Start in strenuous handcrack (5.9) up to a ledge. Move left and continue up four-inch dihedral crack to roof (5.9+). Turn short roof on the right side (5.7). 65 feet.

129   **Ophidiphobia (aka Copperhead) (11–)** ★★★   Same start as *Diet Pepsi*. From the ledge; traverse right (5.9) up to the base of the eight-foot roof with a secure handcrack. Turn the roof via strenuous hand-and-fist jams (5.11–) to a welcome rest at a ledge. Climb the face up and to the left to join *Diet Pepsi* for the last ten feet to the top. This face has one 5.8 move that is tricky to protect. Note: An unexpected surprise was encountered on the first ascent on the ledge above the crux. The name of this route is a suitable

clue as to what was found. 65 feet. FFA: Mike Downing/Scott Hall/ Sandy Fleming 1985.

130   **Team International (11)**   ★★★   Thirty-foot, straight-in fingercrack located on the upper face left of *Flesh & Bone*. Climb thirty feet up clean face past three bolts to the base of finger crack (5.11). Continue up strenuous finger-hand crack (5.10+). When crack ends exit to the left to top out. 70 feet. FA: Bob Scheier (USA)/Bubu Bucek (Czech Republic)/Ornulf Kittelsten (Norway) 12/96. FFA: Clay Frisbie/Bob Scheier 1/97.

131   **Flesh & Bone (9–)**   ★★   Overhanging roof crack system. There are two ways to start this route, both 5.9. The best and most protected alternative is the more distinct fistcrack on the right side. Both starts lead to the overhang with a crack. Turn roof (5.9–) that has a custom-made slot that makes the matter at hand considerably modest. Then follow crack to top. 70 feet.

132   **On the Take (8+)**   ★★   Climb up flakes on the wall right of *Flesh & Bone* and follow them over the bulge to a stance (5.8+). A ramp traverses left near the top of the face to exit. 80 feet. FFA: Scott Hall/Sandy Fleming 1986.

133   **Razorback Roof (9+)**   ★★★★   Located left around corner from *Battle of the Bulge*. Climb up crack thirty feet moderate climbing to an eight-foot triangular roof. Turn the roof via handjams and edges (5.9). Continue in crack system to the crux at the top. This popular route is often done in two pitches to avoid rope drag. 65 feet. FFA: Woody Delp?

134   **Delayed Hand (10+)**   ★   Follow flaring crack up to base of roof. At roof, traverse right (5.9) to obtain next crack system. Move through the flaring roof crack (5.10+). 55 feet. FFA: Bob Scheier 1/97.

COUP D'ÉTAT WALL

135   **Pumpy Love (12– S)**   ★   Climb up middle of wall left of *Battle of the Bulge*. To a large horizontal flake which appears too scary grab but is an intricate part of the climb as a foothold. At the lip of the roof use horizontal crack to reach high positive sloper (5.12–). Turn roof using pumpy jugs and blast to the top. 50 feet. FFA: Mark Wilford 4/91.

136   **Battle of the Bulge (10–)**   ★★★★   Large, right-facing, fist-size dihedral crack. Climb twenty feet up to the roof. Go around roof by fist jams and liebacks (5.10–). Continue up crack to easier climbing up and out. 65 feet.

137   **Coup D'état (10+ PG)**   ★★★★   Mega classic! Thin crack right of *Battle of the Bulge*. Use crack for first twenty feet to turn small roof

(5.10). After that, continue straight up on chickenheads. Strenuous sustained climbing to the top (5.10+). Although no move is above 5.10, the climb has been rated harder because of its sustained nature. This route for many years has stood as a classic testpiece to lead even with the modest rating of 5.10+. 75 feet. Protection: Strenuous to protect, best advice is to be mentally prepared and lead the climb as quickly as possible. If the stance or the hold you are using does not have a good edge, move to the next hold, it will probably be more positive. Leading this route can manifest a feeling much harder than 5.10+ when hanging out placing protection. FFA: Sandy Fleming 1986. [*Coup D'état* reminds me of Jim Karpowitz who has graced the rocks at Sam's Throne for the last couple of decades and is probably responsible for many of the first ascents that are unknown. Jim inspired me to see that climbing is not just about numbers but about using the mind as well as the body to climb. To use experience and smooth climbing techniques, to remain calm in desperate situations, to be able to climb bold demanding routes and also the skill to downclimb or bail out when in trouble on such routes by using a combination of these techniques, the type of climbing that has inspired and given me the most gratification. This style of adventure can be found at any level of climbing. It is this aspect of climbing that has kept this sport vital and exhilarating for me and resulted ultimately in the development of this book.]

138   **Coup de Grâce (10– S)** ★★   Location forty feet right of *Coup D'état.* Follow crack climb up face with path of least resistance through overhang. 75 feet. FFA: Jim Karpowitz 1980s?

139   **Flat Bottom Girls (7)** ★★   Left-arching dihedral crack.

140   **Ode to a Portly Man (11a-d)** ★★★★   Climb up the middle of the distinct orange face with four bolts for protection. A short section of dynamic technical moves leads past the first bolt and a good handhold to clip the second bolt. Above lie positive holds on a slightly overhanging face to create sustained masterful 5.10– playground all the way to the top. After the last bolt follow the row of chickenheads and move up and left following the path of least resistance. This slightly overhung jewel is considerably more sustained than one might assume. Two-bolt anchor. 75 feet. FFA: Frisbie/Schooler/Stites 8/96.

141   **Fat City (7)** ★★   Dihedral crack right of orange face. Climb fifteen feet up to the base of the crack system using both the crack and the jug holds located on either side. When the crack widens to a chimney step right. Fire on large easy holds to top out or squeeze left into the chimney to top out (more difficult). 75 feet.

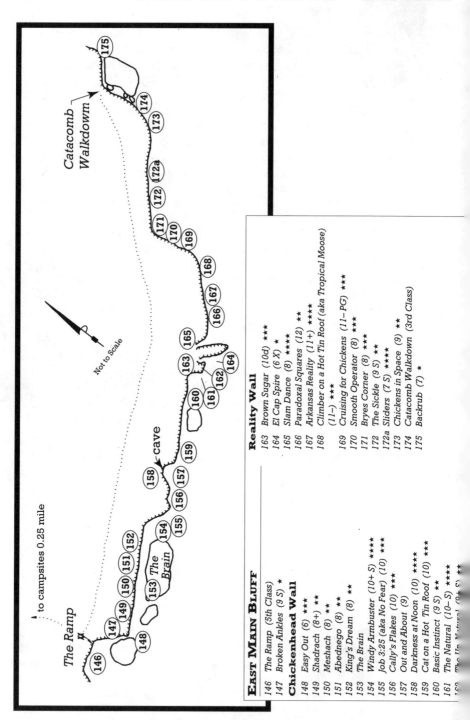

The Ramp

to campsites 0.25 mile

Not to Scale

The Brain

cave

Catacomb Walkdown

EAST MAIN BLUFF

146 The Ramp (5th Class)
147 Broken Ankles (9 S) ★

Chickenhead Wall

148 Easy Out (6) ★★★
149 Shadrach (8+) ★★
150 Meshach (8) ★★
151 Abednego (8) ★★
152 King's Dream (8) ★★
153 The Brain
154 Windy Armbuster (10+ S) ★★★★
155 Job 3:25 (aka No Fear) (10) ★★★
156 Cally's Flakes (10) ★★★
157 Out and About (9)
158 Darkness at Noon (10) ★★★★
159 Cat on a Hot Tin Roof (10) ★★★
160 Basic Instinct (9 S) ★★
161 The Natural (10–S) ★★★★

Reality Wall

163 Brown Sugar (10d) ★★★
164 El Cap Spire (6 X) ★
165 Slam Dance (8) ★★★★
166 Paradoxal Squares (12) ★★
167 Arkansas Reality (11+) ★★★★
168 Climber on a Hot Tin Roof (aka Tropical Moose) (11–) ★★★
169 Cruising for Chickens (11– PG) ★★★
170 Smooth Operator (8) ★★★
171 Bryes Corner (8) ★★★
172 The Sickle (9 S) ★★
172a Sliders (7 S) ★★★★
173 Chickens in Space (9) ★★
174 Catacomb Walkdown (3rd Class)
175 Backrub (7) ★

142   **Cassi's Nightmare (9+)** ★★★   This is a large overhanging
offwidth that slants right. Climb fifteen feet up to where the fist
crack that angles right begins. Have good clean fun for the next
thirty feet using armbars and fistjams till the crack ends (5.9+).
Ascend easy chickenheads (5.5) to the next roof that has a crack
in it. From here there are three options: 1) go directly over roof
through handcrack (5.10) which seems to be the best option to
maximize the climbing on this already excellent route; 2) go
around roof to the right (5.8) to top out; or 3) avoid roof by
traversing left (5.6) to top out. 60 feet.

143   **Fists of Aggression (8)** ★   Nasty roof crack leads to easy
climbing above. 60 feet.

144   **Reptilian (9)** ★★   Climb up twenty feet to roof. Turn roof via
crack (5.9). Continue up crack going to the right in the dihedral
(5.7) and top out. 50 feet.

145   **The Wasp (8)** ★★★   This is the first overhanging crack left of
the ramp. Climb up twenty feet on rotten rock to roof with a crack.
Turn roof and continue in a large, flaring, sustained offwidth. This
is a hardy route with a modest rating, an excellent environment to
hone offwidth skills. 60 feet.

EAST MAIN BLUFF

*The East Bluff can easily be approached from either The Catacomb or The
Ramp Walkdown (which requires some downclimbing). One could also come
in from the Hero Maker trail approach which requires no downclimbing. Both
approaches take ten to twenty minutes from their respective trailheads. From
the Lookout Point on Highway 123 the sharp, well-defined East Bluff line is an
impressive sight. This area is home to some exceptional crack and offwidth
routes. The southeast-facing rock provides protection from the wind and it
radiates the sun's heat, which can raise the temperature by 20 to 30 degrees
on cold winter days.*

146   **The Ramp (5th Class)**   Friction ramp (5.5) to bottom of bluff.
There is a two-bolt anchor located at the top. This is the main
descent route to go to The Throne. Just rappel off anchors and
follow trail into the valley. Many leave a fixed rope on the ramp to
get back up. It is common for many climbers not to use a rope
when accessing *The Ramp*. The sick joke among climbers was
that one of these days a talented climber would fall off after a hard
day of free soloing. There he would be stuck at the bottom with a
couple of broken legs and arms unable to get back up. A week
later someone would find a bloody mess and the climber still

trying to get out. *The Ramp* is an easy climb but it has seen more than a few serious accidents! Fortunately, no fatalities yet. 65 feet.

147   **Broken Ankles (9 S)** ★   Located in the middle of the wall right of *The Ramp*. Start on top of boulder at the base of *The Ramp*; use large pocket move right and continue straight. Protection is crucial after the first move. You might just break your ankles on the slanted boulder below. 40 feet. FFA: Clay Frisbie/Jon Von Canon 1987.

CHICKENHEAD WALL

Wall section scooped out along the bottom with several 5.8 cracks to pull the roof. Rock above has gentle slope (5.4–5.5) filled with various knobs and chickenheads. This seems to be a popular area for top-roping by beginning climbers. 65 feet.

148   **Easy Out (6)** ★★★   Located on the left edge of Chickenhead Wall. Ascend up a little to the right of the edge. Use the path of least resistance continuing straight up. 60 feet.

149   **Shadrach (8+)** ★★   Slab up to handcrack through bulging roof up to Chickenhead Wall. 65 feet.

150   **Meshach (8)** ★★   Slab up to fist crack through bulging roof up to Chickenhead Wall. 65 feet.

151   **Abednego (8)** ★★   Slab up to handcrack through bulging roof up to Chickenhead Wall. 65 feet.

152   **King's Dream (8)** ★★   Slab up and to the right to a crack through bulging roof up to Chickenhead Wall and blast to the top. 65 feet.

153   **The Brain**   Located directly behind Chickenhead Wall. With a bit of imagination the top of this boulder looks like a brain. This is a large boulder that is popular for bouldering. The top of *The Brain* provides another way to gain access to the easier climbing on the Chickenhead Wall.

154   **Windy Armbuster (10+ S)** ★★★★   Prominent face to the right of Chickenhead Wall. This spectacular climb, an Arkansas classic, ascends the middle of the overhanging face. Start the route in the thin thirty-five-foot crack (5.8+). The crux is located in the middle of the route. Continue straight up on strenuous jugs to a shallow cave and finish with the short fistcrack. Get ready for a new set of forearms and a lot of strenuous jug bashing on this overhung masterpiece. This route has been led before, but is generally considered a top-rope classic. This is one of the first 5.10s to be done at Sam's Throne. The first ascent was done in hiking boots! Protection: Tricky to place pro near crux and strenuous to place

above. This could result in a long runout. There is a two-bolt anchor just over the edge from the top for top-roping. 80 feet. FFA: Leroy Scharfenbereg 1976.

155   **Job 3:25 (aka No Fear) (10) ★★★**   Around the corner from Windy Armbuster, orange face with three bolts up steep face. After crux above third bolt, be ready to sling chickenheads. Continue with 5.9 climbing to the top. FFA: Clay Frisbie/Chandler Schooler 1996.

156   **Cally's Flakes (10) ★★★**   Located on the left side of the entrance cave to *Darkness at Noon*. Boulder up (5.10) through orange rock twenty feet to gain access to the crack system. The rock quality at the bottom is better than it appears, but still be careful of loose rock. Follow the hand/fist crack for some awkward moves that are well protected.

157   **Out and About (9)**   Start in the entrance of the cave, ascend right face to large roof crack (5.6). At the roof, traverse right to the corner of the roof. Move around the roof by means of the face and crack (5.9). Continue up on the dihedral crack. 65 feet. FFA: Clay Frisbie 1991.

158   **Darkness at Noon (10) ★★★★**   Located in wet cave around the corner from *Windy Armbuster*. Tucked away in the back of this cave is one of the best crack climbs in Arkansas. Reminiscent of Utah, this handcrack ascends to the top of the cave, thirty-five feet. **(P1)** Ascend strenuous sustained handcrack to the top of the cave thirty-five feet to a hanging two-bolt belay (5.10). **(P2)** If you like caving you will enjoy this pitch. Begin from hanging belay and traverse straight out of the cave by using a thin ledge for your feet. As soon as possible, stem across using both walls. Continue the traverse by squeezing through the narrow section in the top of the cave (5.8 to 5.10 depending on body size, weird). Proceed to the outside of the cave and set up a belay. **(P3)** At the roof, traverse right to the corner of the roof. Move around the corner by means of using face and crack (5.9). Continue up on the dihedral crack. Bring many cam units; they might come in handy. It might be beneficial to bring a headlamp too. 35 feet up, 65 feet out, 40 feet up. FFA: Clay Frisbie/Woody Delp 1990.

159   **Cat on a Hot Tin Roof (10) ★★★**   Obvious fistcrack (5.7) leads thirty feet up to an eight-foot overhanging roof with a handcrack. Turn roof (5.10) by means of handjams, edging, and whatever else might work. Belay above roof. Second pitch follows large crack to the top (5.6). This route is a good introductory course to *Arkansas Reality*. 70 feet. FFA: Craig Thomas or Jim Karpowitz?

160   **Basic Instinct (9 S)** ★★   This route climbs a slightly overhanging face about seventy feet left of *The Natural*. When walking from *Cat on a Hot Tin Roof*, scramble up a smooth boulder in the trail. When the trail levels off and before it heads back down the hill, begin on overhanging face. Continue up on no positive holds and minimal protection. 60 feet. FFA: Gary Olsen 4/92.

161   **The Natural (10– S)** ★★★★   This is a breathtaking arête. Start by climbing up the sixty-five-foot arête (5.9). Located near the top of the route is the crux (5.10–). Protection is tricky, lots of slings to loop chickenheads might be helpful. 80 feet. FFA: Jim Karpowitz.

162   **The Un-Natural (9+ S)** ★★   This route climbs the arête just right of *The Natural*. Begin by following the good crack up to the roof where the crack ends and the protection possibilities are real poor. Then climb the arête all the way up to the top. The crux is the bulging section of rock. At this point the pro becomes marginal. 60 feet. FFA: Gary Olsen/Leah Appel 4/92.

163   **Brown Sugar (10d)** ★★★   Located on the left side of the prow. Start in the middle of the brown-colored wall moving up and to the right. Taking the path of least resistance, crux is reached just below where the rock changes color below the overhang. Above overhang, jugbash (5.7) forty feet to a ledge where you can exit the route two ways: 1) climb directly past the bolt through the overhang (5.10+) for another interesting crux move; or 2) move to the left and continue a 5.7 jugbash to the top. Four bolts, two-bolt anchor. 65 feet. FFA: Clay Frisbie/Chandler Schooler 1996.

REALITY WALL

164   **El Cap Spire (6 X)** ★   Chimney right of the prow. Start on the outside edge of the two-foot chimney, move up and toward the inside of The Catacomb. Continue in the middle of the chimney all the way to the top. The best source of protection is good technique. 60 feet.

165   **Slam Dance (8)** ★★★★   Located in the back of the cave right of the prow, is a perfect dihedral handcrack that is twenty feet long (5.8) up to a ledge. The remaining part of the route is offwidth (5.6). This route is fantastic for practicing hand-and-foot jam technique. 70 feet.

166   **Paradoxal Squares (12)** ★★   The most impressive feature of this climb is the nasty looking, body-size offwidth crack located above the roof. Begin route by moderate climbing twenty feet up to the base of where the roof with a thin crack begins. At roof use dyno face moves to slam in a handjam at the lip of the roof (5.12). At the lip, a killer footjam can provide time to hang upside down and place protection and maybe even chalk up before diving into the offwidth. Turn roof by squeezing into the offwidth (5.11). This

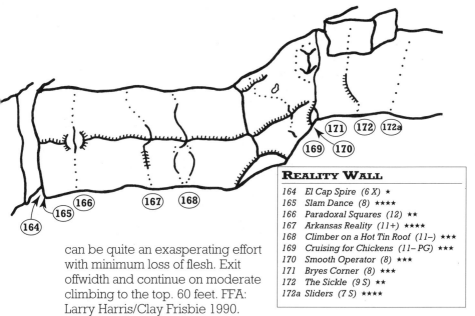

REALITY WALL

164	El Cap Spire (6 X) ★
165	Slam Dance (8) ★★★★
166	Paradoxal Squares (12) ★★
167	Arkansas Reality (11+) ★★★★
168	Climber on a Hot Tin Roof (11–) ★★★
169	Cruising for Chickens (11– PG) ★★★
170	Smooth Operator (8) ★★★
171	Bryes Corner (8) ★★★
172	The Sickle (9 S) ★★
172a	Sliders (7 S) ★★★★

can be quite an exasperating effort with minimum loss of flesh. Exit offwidth and continue on moderate climbing to the top. 60 feet. FFA: Larry Harris/Clay Frisbie 1990.

167 **Arkansas Reality (11+)** ★★★★ Intended only for the mentally disturbed who enjoy Arkansas cracks at their best. Climb fifteen feet up sloping face and begin fingercrack (5.9) up to the roof. Begin twelve-foot strenuous overhung crack by means of deep hand-and-fist jams. Continue with handjams or whatever works best for you over the roof (5.11). Set up comfortable belay above the roof. Finish climb above on (5.5) jugs, forty feet. Still this route stands as a testpiece for aspiring hardman crack climbers. Pitch one: 40 feet; Pitch two: 40 more easy feet. [My first experience on this route (falling many times only part of the way up) was with Craig Thomas. For many years Craig made a yearly pilgrimage to Sam's Throne to red point *Arkansas Reality*. Craig epitomizes what Arkansas rock climbing is about. With his tall, gaunt structure shod in an old T-shirt and mechanic pants, he would scale some of the hardest, gnarliest, scariest crack climbs in Northern Arkansas—many with just hex nuts for protection. With his uncanny brutal ability to climb, he maintains a humility and modesty even when among the most novice of climbers. With a thick southern accent and friendly nature, he would likely befriend or help whomever he might encounter. Well, both Craig and this route lured me into the domain of crack climbing. Later, after more than four dozen times up this route (most excursions to enjoy the night), I can honestly say I learned what a handjam is, and that *Arkansas Reality* is still one of my all time favorite routes.] FA: Jim Karpowitz? FFA: Jim Karpowitz or Craig Thomas? 1980s.

The notorious Craig Thomas on Arkansas Reality (5.11+) ★★★★, East Main Bluff. Photo: Billy Bisswanger.

168   **Climber on a Hot Tin Roof (aka Tropical Moose) (11–)** ★★★
A thin crack runs through a roof located twenty feet right of
Arkansas Reality. Use either crack to reach the base of the roof
(5.8). (Both cracks have rotten rock. The left crack is more
preferable.) Turn roof reaching for good handjams and jugholds
(5.9+). You might catch some dynamic air turning this roof. Above
roof, the crack widens to a fist size. The next fifteen feet are
strenuous (5.11–). A good footlock, heelhook or kneejam is
essential to lessen the strain. Then continue on moderate climbing
to the top. 60 feet. FFA: Craig Thomas/Billy Bisswinger 1985.

169   **Cruising for Chickens (11– PG)** ★★★   Located thirty feet left of
Smooth Operator. This hair-raising climb begins in a two-inch
shallow crack climb twenty feet up to a five-foot roof (5.9). A short
handcrack is located above the lip of the roof. Turn the roof via
the crack reaching for holds above the crack (5.11–). Continue
the line by face climbing following the thin discontinuous crack
that angles up and left (5.9 weird). The crux does protect well, but
it is strenuous to place. The rest of the climb, protection is there
but it might be hard to spot and weird to find the right placement.
For those who enjoy adventurous leading, this is a good climb to
carry a lot of gear on. 60 feet. FFA: Clay Frisbie/Woody Delp
1989.

170   **Smooth Operator (8)** ★★★   Dihedral corner, fifty yards west of
Catacomb Walkdown. Start in a twenty-foot fistcrack left of
dihedral. The crack angles back toward dihedral corner (5.8).
Continue in dihedral on left side of rock column (5.7). 60 feet.

171   **Bryes Corner (8)** ★★★   Climb gently sloping dihedral corner
and stay in handcrack system on the left (5.8). Sustained all the
way to the top. This seems to be a favorite top-rope area for
novice climbers. 55 feet.

172   **The Sickle (9 S)** ★★   Face climb located twenty feet right of
Bryes Corner. Climb up easy friction slab twenty-five feet to a
twenty-foot vertical headwall. Climb middle of headwall starting
on the sickle-shaped rock (5.9). It is tricky to protect the crux on
the headwall. 55 feet. FFA: Robin Coleman 1990.

172a   **Sliders (7 S)** ★★★★   Friction climb (5.7) twenty feet to obtain
positive holds on slab, continue with moderate climbing.

173   **Chickens in Space (9)** ★★   Thin crack located thirty feet left of
Catacomb Walkdown that winds its way up the face. Moderate
climbing leads to the crux at the top. 50 feet. FFA: Woody Delp
1988.

174   **Catacomb Walkdown (3rd Class)**   Located 400 yards east of
The Ramp. This is a ramp of large jumbled blocks for the first

thirty feet down. Then descend down a short chimney (catacomb) onto a block. Exit by crawling out of catacomb under large stuck boulder (it hasn't fallen down yet). This is an easier walkdown than the ramp. Also, this is the best way to bring children and dogs down without taking a much greater walk. 55 feet.

175   **Backrub (7)** ★   Dihedral crack to the right around the corner from *Catacomb Walkdown*. A small tree is located directly behind the crack. One may use the tree as another means of pro or as a way to rest by leaning back against it while climbing. Fist-size dihedral crack with nice jugs on either side of the dihedral. Top out next to *Catacomb Walkdown*. 35 feet.

DEAD DOG WALL

176   **Whiff of Dead Dog (10+)** ★★★   Large offwidth that goes through overhang (5.10+). Continue crack in an easy dihedral (5.8). It's time to get physical. 50 feet. Note: This can be protected by climbing inside the chimney and placing pro before doing the crux. FFA: Clay Frisbie/Mike Davison 1990.

177   **Dead Dog (11–)** ★★★★   Located thirty feet right of *Whiff of Dead Dog* next to a tree. Start this strenuous armbuster just left of the tree. After mounting the rock, move a few feet to the right of the tree and start up the face. Continue straight up the face to the top. This route has been retrobolted with two bolts added between the first and second pin. This route is not an easy clip-and-go route as it might appear; some tricky pro placements keep things interesting at the top. This route was not named after dogs that have taken the big tumble, but rather what might happen if you miss the second clip before the bolts were added. Two fixed pins, three bolts, and a two-bolt anchor. 75 feet. FFA: Clay Frisbie/Woody Delp 1990.

DEAD DOG WALL

176   *Whiff of Dead Dog (10+)* ★
177   *Dead Dog (11–)* ★★★★
178   *Akimbo (10+ S-X)* ★★
179   *Renewed Mind (9)* ★★★
180   *Mindless (8)*
181   *Dunamis (8)* ★★

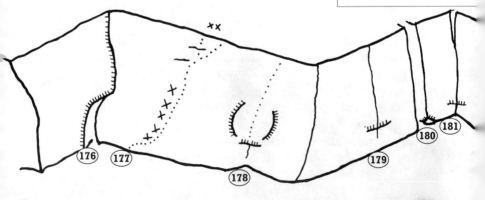

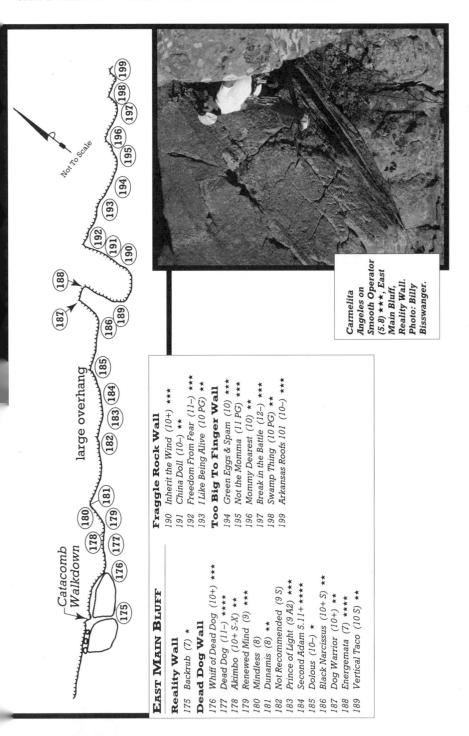

Not To Scale

Catacomb Walkdown

large overhang

Carmelita Angeles on Smooth Operator (5.8) ★★★, East Main Bluff, Reality Wall. Photo: Billy Bisswanger.

EAST MAIN BLUFF

Reality Wall
175 *Backrub* (7) ★

Dead Dog Wall
176 *Whiff of Dead Dog* (10+) ★★★
177 *Dead Dog* (11–) ★★★★
178 *Akimbo* (10+ S-X) ★★
179 *Renewed Mind* (9) ★★★
180 *Mindless* (8)
181 *Dunamis* (8) ★★
182 *Not Recommended* (9 S)
183 *Prince of Light* (9 A2) ★★★
184 *Second Adam 5.11+* ★★★★
185 *Dolous* (10–) ★
186 *Black Narcissus* (10+ S) ★★
187 *Dog Warrior* (10+) ★★
188 *Energemata* (7) ★★★★
189 *Vertical Taco* (10 S) ★★

Fraggle Rock Wall
190 *Inherit the Wind* (10+) ★★★
191 *China Doll* (10–) ★★
192 *Freedom From Fear* (11–) ★★★
193 *I Like Being Alive* (10 PG) ★★

Too Big To Finger Wall
194 *Green Eggs & Spam* (10) ★★★
195 *Not the Momma* (11 PG) ★★★
196 *Mommy Dearest* (10) ★★
197 *Break in the Battle* (12–) ★★★
198 *Swamp Thing* (10 PG) ★★
199 *Arkansas Roofs 101* (10–) ★★★

178   **Akimbo (10+ S-X)** ★★   Located seventy-five feet right of *Dead Dog*. Climb up soft red sandstone thirty feet to a short roof (5.8). Pull the roof (5.10+) above. Continue straight up the twisted looking face using chickenheads (5.9). Questionable protection on bad rock up to the roof. After the roof the pro is good. 65 feet. FFA: Jim Karpowitz 1989.

179   **Renewed Mind (9)** ★★★   This apparent crack line has a lone pine tree at the top of the route. Climb ten feet up to an overhanging hand-size crack. Turn the bulge with some strenuous moves. Continue in crack which turns into a large, dark, watergroove with moderate climbing. 45 feet.

180   **Mindless (8)**   Chimney/offwidth. 45 feet.

181   **Dunamis (8)** ★★   Roof crack in the corner. A boulder roof crack problem leads to fifty feet of moderate climbing. 55 feet.

182   **Not Recommended (9 S)**   Ledge system that leads to first belay point on *Second Adam*. Climb fifteen feet up and traverse right on rotten rock to the start of the ledge system. Scoot, slither and slide across ledge. The ledge then becomes a horizontal crack that leads to belay anchors (5.9). 50 feet sideways, 35 feet up. FFA: Clay Frisbie 11/94.

183   **Prince of Light (9 A2)** ★★★   Free climb or aid first pitch of *Second Adam* (5.10 A0). From this point, continue with the second pitch up to the roof. Then start aid climbing in the crack that runs horizontally to the left over the big hole. This part of the route provides some excellent aid climbing that requires only a couple of pin placements (one short KB and LA or BA). After aiding through big roof system, start free climbing up large jugs (5.9) to a point where a belay can be set up halfway up the face. Long slings are needed to loop large horns for the belay. Third pitch, traverse left thirty feet to a dihedral crack (5.9) to top out. Not only is this a great aid climb, it is also a way to find out what is in the big hole. Originally done at night, it provided splendid entertainment for a cold winter night. 100+ feet! FA: Clay Frisbie/Tom Hancock 11/94.

184   **Second Adam (11+)** ★★★★   This is one of the few two-pitch routes, and possibly the longest route at Sam's Throne. It is a massive fifty-foot overhung roof system that has a large hole on the left wall under the roof. The first pitch is a sport route that ascends the orange overhung arête (5.11+) past five bolts up to belay anchors, forty feet. The second (best) pitch follows the dihedral crack (5.10) to the base of the roof; then traverses right along wide crack past one bolt (5.10). At the end of the traverse a total leglock can be obtained to clip the next bolt and set up for

turning the lip of the roof (5.11). This route was the dream child of eight years of speculation as to the possibility of weaving a route through the massive roof system. The second pitch of this route provides an immense deal of adventure and exposure with a wide variety of offwidths, cracks, heel hooks and dynamic moves to satisfy the strongest of appetites. Bring numerous long slings and a mixed rack for the second pitch. 70 feet. FFA: Frisbie/Caughlin/Hancock 11/94.

185 **Dolous (10–)** ★ A flaring chimney offwidth dihedral with black rock covered in green moss. This route is normally wet; a good place to avoid the summer sun and heat. 55 feet. FFA: Clay Frisbie/Kevin Hale 2/95.

186 **Black Narcissus (10+ S)** ★★ Vertical black stain located on a rounded arête with a thin intermittent crack system that runs through a short overhang. 60 feet. FFA: Clay Frisbie/Tom Hancock 3/94.

187 **Dog Warrior (10+)** ★★ Eternally wet, mossy, overhanging fistcrack in the left corner. Start route halfway back in cave; weird stems to obtain wet mossy roof crack. Turn roof with bizarre moves (5.10+ weird). Continue on to the top with a couple more tricky moves. Even with the wetness and mossy crack, this route is still an unforgettable experience. 45 feet. FFA: Clay Frisbie/Tom Hancock 2/95.

188 **Energemata (7)** ★★★★ Offwidth chimney crack in right corner. Start in the back of the chimney moving up and left; moderate climbing leads to a nice handcrack (5.7).

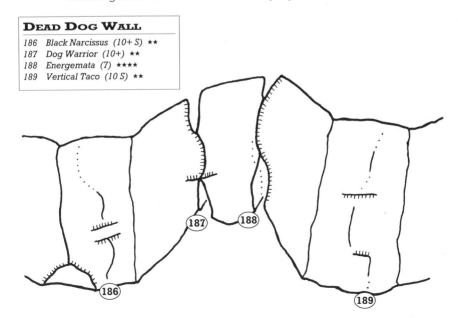

DEAD DOG WALL

186 *Black Narcissus (10+ S)* ★★
187 *Dog Warrior (10+)* ★★
188 *Energemata (7)* ★★★★
189 *Vertical Taco (10 S)* ★★

189   **Vertical Taco (10 S)** ★★   A twenty-foot handcrack located in the middle of the route is the most obvious feature. Start up rounded arête directly across from *Black Narcissus* moving up and left to a protruding block. Turn the overhang (5.10–) to gain access to the handcrack. The crack ends at a ledge; continue up and right on the arête (5.10) using some very questionable holds and protection. 60 feet. FFA: Tom Hancock/Pat Murphy 10/93.

FRAGGLE ROCK WALL

190   **Inherit the Wind (10+)** ★★★   Face climb on orange rock in the center of wall. Five bolts, one fixed pin; need stoppers and long runners to loop chickenheads at the top. 65 feet. FFA: Clay Frisbie/Merick Poplawski 2/95.

191   **China Doll (10–)** ★★   Climb in dihedral roof crack avoiding loose rock. Turn roof by using good handcrack. After roof, continue to top on moderate climbing. 55 feet. FFA: Clay Frisbie/Woody Delp 1990.

192   **Freedom From Fear (11–)** ★★★   Obvious left-arching roof crack line. A sometimes wet, (5.9) left-facing dihedral crack leads to a left-arching roof crack. Turn lip of roof (5.11–), follow crack and offwidth to top. 50 feet. FFA: Clay Frisbie/Jon Von Canon 1990.

193   **I Like Being Alive (10 PG)** ★★   Located twenty feet right of *Freedom from Fear*. Start up gently sloping orange face with a thin shallow crack (tricky and strenuous to protect) that leads to a roof with a thin crack. At the lip of the roof the crack widens to hand size. After turning the roof, continue straight up and to the right.

Fraggle Rock Wall
190 *Inherit the Wind (10+)* ★★★
191 *China Doll (10–)* ★★
192 *Freedom From Fear (11–)* ★★★
193 *I Like Being Alive (10 PG)* ★★

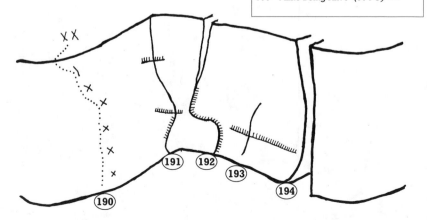

[Driving down to Sam's, Woody and I were sideswiped and missed a head on collision at 65 miles an hour in heavy traffic. Only mere millimeters were the difference between being planted six feet under ground and still breathing. Wouldn't you know it, we jumped on this heart-thumping route while our brief glimpse of the grim reaper was still fresh in our minds. Needless to say, this route was a piece of cake, mentally, compared to our ride down. The warm rock under my fingertips, the smell of fresh pine mingled with the musty, pungent odor of sandstone and the sweet fellowship of other climbers and friends gathered about. Enjoying yet another day watching the magnanimous yellow ball rise and wane were welcome reminders that I like being alive! It also brought back the startling reality that riding in an automobile is always dangerous.] 75 feet. FFA: Frisbie/Delp/Denis Nelms 10/91.

TOO BIG TO FINGER WALLS

Tired of face climbing? Are your fingers and elbow tendons tweaked from cranking on mono doights and crimper holds. Maybe you just want to hone your skills at squeezing, grunting and using all sorts of body parts to perform weird jams. Well, you are at the right area because the next four climbs listed are all offwidth climbs. That's right, the weird, wacky, world of offwidths. If you come, come prepared because these routes don't accept Visa or American Express; but they do accept mammoth cams and tube chocks (big boy toys).

194   **Green Eggs & Spam (10)** ★★★   Conspicuous elongated offwidth crack, this route seems improbable to protect but actually accepts a wide variety of smaller protection devices. One large cam (Big Dude) is very advantageous to have when protecting the crux section. 60 feet. FFA: Frisbie/Hancock/Murphy/Eric Massey/Kevin Hale 7/94.

195   **Not the Momma (11 PG)** ★★★   If one scrutinizes the east bluff line from the lookout point on Highway 123, the top section of this route is an extremely distinct crack line. This route is a large crack that varies from six-inches to one-foot wide. Start climb by chimneying up to a short bomb bay chimney and squeeze through this section (5.10+) to gain access to the outside of the offwidth. Continue up several feet to a large incut ledge to encounter the crux section. At this point the crack narrows to six inches with the wall being smooth on either side of the crack. This is a good place to see if a large tube chock or a large cam unit really do work. Without these items, climbing this monster crack could become quite an intense endeavor. If you like offwidth

climbing and have the right toys this is a jewel of a route. 80 feet. FFA: Clay Frisbie/Tom Hancock 1991.

196   **Mommy Dearest (10)** ★★   Terminally wet offwidth in right-facing, overhanging, black dihedral located just right of *Not the Momma*. When leading, chimney up and preplace protection from above (5.7 PG) before moving back down and out to tackle the offwidth/roof. There is an alternative to this route: climb through the chimney and don't do the 5.10 overhang. This makes for an interesting serious 5.8 chimney—a good warmup for "The Texas Flake" on *The Nose*, El Capitan. 80 feet. FFA: Chuck Caughlin/Tom Hancock 10/93.

197   **Break in the Battle (12–)** ★★★   This route offers a mix of all kinds of climbing i.e. crack, face and offwidth. Start on the orange face (5.8) to the base of the six-foot roof with a bolt located just below where the crack begins. Turn the roof using various forms of climbing (5.12–). A few feet of easy climbing leads to the next roof (5.11–) to top out. 70 feet, 75 feet. FFA: Frisbie/Von Canon/Hancock/Delp 1991.

198   **Swamp Thing (10 PG)** ★★   Significant dihedral crack system in orange rock that slightly overhangs. The crux, located in the middle of the route, is usually wet. A pool of water is located in a little cave back under where the route begins. Dripping water can many times be heard coming out of the cave. 65 feet. FFA: Clay Frisbie/Hancock 1991.

199   **Arkansas Roofs 101 (10–)** ★★★   A great beginner course in 5.10 roof climbing with one well protected 5.10 move. Fistcrack with large pockets and edges; twenty feet of moderate climbing leads to roof. Turn roof using crack and edges (5.10–). Continue in (5.8) crack to top. 50 feet. FFA: Jon Von Canon 3/91.

READER'S DIGEST WALLS

199a   **Beggar's Palm (10+ TR)** ★★   Climb arête face.

200   **Reader's Digest Condensed (10)** ★★★★   Thin left-angling crack system just right of the dihedral. This route may be short but is power packed for its length. A weird mount (5.10) starts the route. Continue in system with a series of 5.9+ moves to the top. 35 feet. FFA: Clay Frisbie/Woody Delp 3/91.

201   **Points to Ponder (9)** ★★   Short, overhanging dihedral crack with less than positive holds on each wall. 35 feet. FFA: Clay Frisbie 3/91.

202   **Purple Pinky Blues (11+)** ★★   If you like pumpy, overhanging, weird crack climbs, this is it. Climb up orange face on questionable flakes (5.9+) to a finger-size crack that cuts the roof.

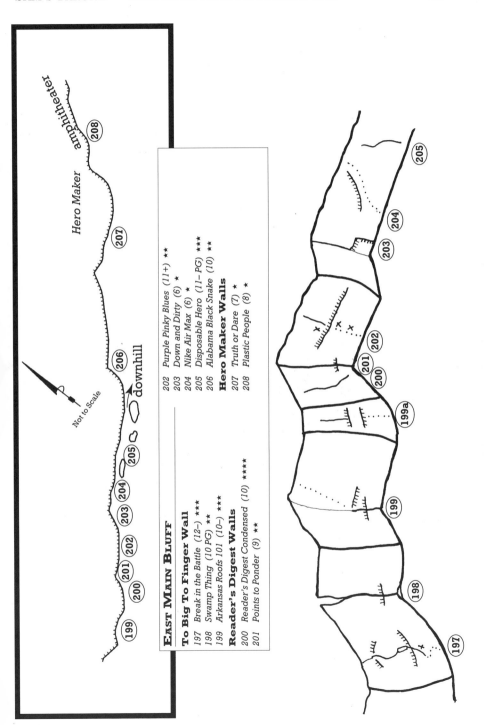

East Main Bluff

To Big To Finger Wall

197 Break in the Battle (12–) ★★★
198 Swamp Thing (10 PG) ★★
199 Arkansas Roofs 101 (10–) ★★★

Reader's Digest Walls

200 Reader's Digest Condensed (10) ★★★★
201 Points to Ponder (9) ★★

202 Purple Pinky Blues (11+) ★★
203 Down and Dirty (6) ★
204 Nike Air Max (6) ★
205 Disposable Hero (11– PG) ★★★
206 Alabama Black Snake (10) ★★

Hero Maker Walls

207 Truth or Dare (7) ★
208 Plastic People (8) ★

An awkward handcrack while heelhooking to turn the bulge
(5.11+) makes for a unique crux. Mixed cams smaller than one
inch, two bolts, one pin. 45 feet. FFA: Clay Frisbie 3/96.

203 **Down and Dirty (6)** ★   Right-facing dihedral with fistcrack and
a large ledge located halfway up. This is an easy way to gain
access to the top to the bluff. 35 feet.

204 **Nike Air Max (6)** ★   Right diagonal crack with large flakes
surrounding the underneath side of the crack. 35 feet.

205 **Disposable Hero (11– PG)** ★★★   Just before going down the
hill, a noticeable left-leaning, thin crack system situated between
large boulders. Many 5.10 moves with the crux at the top make
this plainly a harder version of *Reader's Digest*. Tricky pro
placements at the top. 40 feet. FFA: Clay Frisbie/Tom Hancock
7/94.

206 **Alabama Black Snake (10)** ★★   Black slab leads to winding
handcrack. FFA: Clay Frisbie/Tom Hancock 1994.

*Eric Forney on Second Adam (5.11+) ★★★★,
East Main Bluff, Dead Dog Wall. Photo: Ladd
Campbell.*

HERO MAKER WALL

The Hero Maker area encompasses the east-most end of Mt. Judea. There are several ways to get there. The easiest approach is from the horsetrail walkdown (a ten-minute approach) or follow the wall around from the east bluff from the catacomb Walkdown. The horsetrail is one of the easiest ways into the valley that houses the Sam's Throne area because it requires no technical decent and supplies a good trail. This is one of the best ways to bring in dogs or children. Many also find the horsetrail a superb mountain bike trail. Hero Maker is a relatively small area, the west side of which has a large impressive amphitheater and the center contains the impressive overhang of Hero Maker Wall. Hero Maker Wall is capped by a spectacular forty-foot roof that is outlined by two striking crack systems that provided not only a bizarre feature to gaze upon but some of the most interesting routes at Sam's Throne.

207   **Truth or Dare (7)** ★   Weird crack system near edge of drop-off. 50 feet.

208   **Plastic People (8)** ★   Located on left wall of the amphitheater. Ascend up the left side of the gently sloping wall on lichen-covered knobs (5.6) with no protection. At top of wall continue in dihedral crack (5.8). 50 feet.

209   **Lust not Love (10+ PG)** ★★   Same start *Smoke in Your Eyes.* Before the vertical dihedral, traverse left and up toward arête with one bolt and continue straight up (5.10+). Was top-roped once before being lead. 60 feet. FFA: Woody Delp 1990.

210   **Smoke in Your Eyes (9–)** ★★★★   Start route on moderate 5.7 ramp with a prominent left-facing dihedral crack for forty feet. Near the top crack turns vertical containing excellent 5.9– moves. Finish the route by turning a short roof. 60 feet. FFA: Clay Frisbie/Woody Delp 3/91.

211   **Are The Dead Alive Now? No (12 TR)** ★★   Overhanging face right of *Smoke in Your Eyes.* 70 feet.

212   **Second Hand Hero (10)** ★★★★   This classic route contains some excellent sustained 5.9+ climbing all the way up fifty feet to the roof. This is the crack system on the left of Hero Maker Wall. Start the route by climbing in the crack up to the base of the pillar. Then climb pillar to the onset of the roof. Turn roof to top out climb (5.10). 75 feet. FFA: Jon Von Canon/Clay Frisbie 1990.

213   **First Hand Hero (10+ PG)** ★★★★   Located on the right side of Hero Maker Wall, this is the route that looks impossible (or so we assumed). With a twenty-foot overhanging roof crack at the top, this route is not quite as arduous as it would seem. A pool of stagnant water usually resides not far from where this route

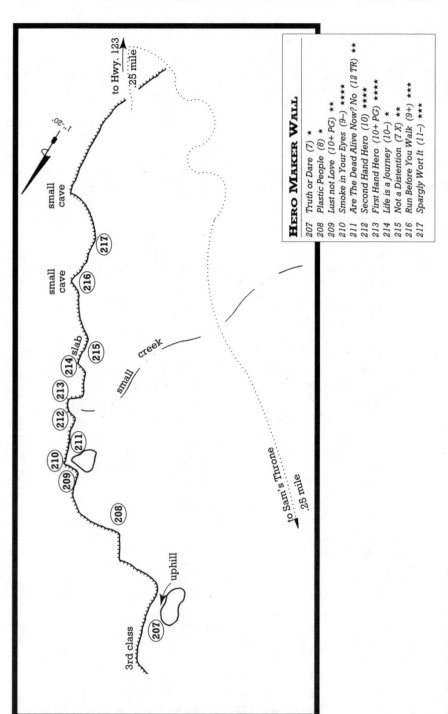

HERO MAKER WALL

207 Truth or Dare (7) ★
208 Plastic People (8) ★
209 Lust not Love (10+ PG) ★★
210 Smoke in Your Eyes (9−) ★★★★
211 Are The Dead Alive Now? No (12 TR) ★★
212 Second Hand Hero (10) ★★★★
213 First Hand Hero (10+ PG) ★★★★
214 Life is a Journey (10−) ★
215 Not a Distention (7 X) ★★
216 Run Before You Walk (9+) ★★★
217 Spargly Wort It (11−) ★★★

begins. Start route by climbing twenty feet(5.9) up to an easy stance on a slab. Most times this slab is wet or soggy. If it is wet, just use direct aid for one or two moves (don't distress you didn't miss anything unless you aid the rest of the route) to achieve the nice dry vertical crack with a bolt to the right. The free climbing begins from the bolt. Take the vertical lieback crack on the right fifteen feet (5.10). Continue up crack system twenty feet (5.10) to roof. Climb under impressive roof via great handjams with commendable exposure and turn roof to top out (5.10+). This route may not make you a hero, but it will provide an interesting adventure. 80 feet. FFA: Clay Frisbie/Jon Von Canon 1990.

214 **Life is a Journey (10–)** ★   Offwidth chimney crack next to slab. Moderate 5.7 climbing in the chimney leads to roof crack near top. Awkward moves (5.10–) lead to top. 60 feet. FFA: Clay Frisbie 1993.

215 **Not a Distention (7 X)** ★★   Meander up slab topping out at large tree. This route offers no real protection but enjoyable climbing. 60 feet.

216 **Run Before You Walk (9+)** ★★★   Located in the cave one hundred yards to the right and around the corner from *First Hand Hero*. This is a massive roof system with about one hundred feet of overhang but the climbing is much more moderate than it appears. Start in very back of the cave where the crack system starts. Boulder 5.10 the first ten feet of the route up to a ledge to gain access to the roof. From ledge follow the roof via traversing offwidth moves out and around the first roof (5.9+). After first roof continue moderate climbing. Second roof top out with 5.9+ move. 70 feet. FFA: Jon Von Canon/Clay Frisbie 3/91.

217 **Spargly Wort It (11–)** ★★★   Crack twenty feet right of cave. Ten feet off the ground is a right-facing, slightly overhanging dihedral crack. The route starts by manteling up over the roof to gain access to the crack. The first ascent started the climb by stacking a pile of rocks to reach the lip of the overhang where the route begins. Another tactic used was to place a large cam in the crack above by placing it taped to a cheater stick. This was to protect the otherwise unprotectable and precarious start. Sounds kind of like sport climbing tactics without the bolts! Note: A nice handcrack that narrows to fingers boulder problem is located under the start of this route. Maybe someday a new generation of climbers will be able to start this climb at the boulder problem and connect it up to go all the way, doubtless to be on the extreme edge of climbing. 80 feet. FFA: Frisbie/Hancock/Davidson 11/93.

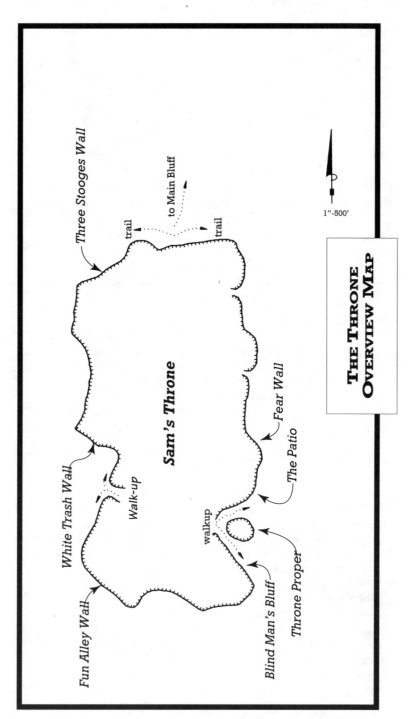

THE THRONE (SAM'S THRONE)

Sam's Throne or The Throne as most call it, sports a very high quality rock and has the largest number of well-established popular climbs in the area. The Throne is the cap of rock that is clearly visible from the Lookout Point on Highway 123 and from The Ramp on the Main bluff. From the Ramp it is an easy ten-minute approach. One can walk around the entire cap of The Throne with its fifty routes in less than half an hour. Climbing is good year round with south-facing walls in winter and trees to provide shade in the summer. The routes here are steep and pumpy. Many of them are top-rope classics because of the ease with which top ropes can be set up in this area.

Routes are described starting from the trailhead and working clockwise around The Throne.

SOUTH SIDE

218a Chimney (6)   The cave is located 100 yards left of trailhead. Obvious chimney crack that starts with a short face climb to begin the chimney. 50 feet.

218 Short & Sweet (7) ★★   Climb fifteen feet up to the twenty-foot handcrack and enjoy. Protection might be tricky at the start. 35 feet. FFA: Paul "Goose" Giesenhagen 1989.

219 Quantum Leap (12– TR)   Overhanging curved face that is close to the ground. The climb consists of lunging for large pockets while moving right. This can make for a bad pendulum fall on top-rope because of a large boulder that is located right in the line of fire. 35 feet.

220 Chuck's Crack (10 PG) ★   Broken crack system to the right of *Skank Master* on the edge between *Hitchhiker* and *Quantum Leap*. Strenuous crack start. Follow the crack straight up twenty feet to a horizontal crack, then traverse right for exit. This route is strenuous to protect. 45 feet.

221 Skank Master (11 PG) ★★★   Face climb with bolt located fifteen feet up. Above bolt, move up and to the right using path of least resistance (5.9+). The middle of the route is tricky to protect. 60 feet. FFA: Clay Frisbie/Woody Delp 9/91.

222 Hitchhiker (10+ S) ★★   Located twenty feet right of *Eminence Front*, ten feet right of chimney. Start up orange face climbing left on large, detached flake twenty feet. Then move right five feet reaching for a block that looks like a thumb (loose rock). From the thumb, move left under the small roof with a bolt (5.10+) and continue straight up. Protection runs out after the bolt. A ¾-x-4-inch pocket provides reasonable pro. 55 feet. FFA: Clay Frisbie/Chuck Foster 1989.

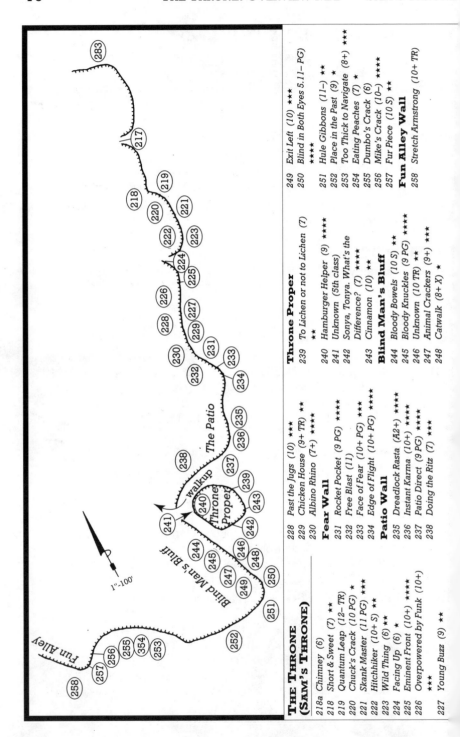

THE THRONE (SAM'S THRONE)

218a Chimney (6)
218 Short & Sweet (7) ★★
219 Quantum Leap (12– TR)
220 Chuck's Crack (10 PG) ★
221 Skank Master (11 PG) ★★★
222 Hitchhiker (10+ S) ★★
223 Wild Thing (6) ★★
224 Facing Up (6) ★
225 Eminent Front (10+) ★★★★
226 Overpowered by Funk (10+) ★★★
227 Young Buzz (9) ★★

228 Past the Jugs (10) ★★★
229 Chicken House (9+ TR) ★★
230 Albino Rhino (7+) ★★★★

Fear Wall
231 Rocket Pocket (9 PG) ★★★★
232 Free Blast (11)
233 Face of Fear (10+ PG) ★★★
234 Edge of Flight (10+ PG) ★★★★

Patio Wall
235 Dreadlock Rasta (A2+) ★★★★
236 Instant Karma (10+) ★★★★
237 Patio Direct (9 PG) ★★★★
238 Doing the Ritz (7) ★★★

Throne Proper
239 To Lichen or not to Lichen (7) ★★
240 Hamburger Helper (9) ★★★★
241 Unknown (5th class)
242 Sonya, Tonya, What's the Difference? (7) ★★★★
243 Cinnamon (10) ★★

Blind Man's Bluff
244 Bloody Bowels (10 S) ★★
245 Bloody Knuckles (9 PG) ★★★★
246 Unknown (10 TR) ★★
247 Animal Crackers (9+) ★★★
248 Catwalk (8+ X) ★

249 Exit Left (10) ★★★
250 Blind in Both Eyes 5.11– PG) ★★★★
251 Hule Gibbons (11–) ★★
252 Place in the Past (9) ★
253 Too Thick to Navigate (8+) ★★★
254 Eating Peaches (7) ★
255 Dumbo's Crack (6)
256 Mike's Crack (10–) ★★★★
257 Fur Piece (10 S) ★★

Fun Alley Wall
258 Stretch Armstrong (10+ TR)

223 **Wild Thing (6)** ★★   Same start as *Hitchhiker*. Start up orange face climbing left on large flake 20 feet. Traverse left on ledge to the chimney. At the chimney, climb the left face straight up the path of least resistance. Another variation is to climb up the chimney (5.5). 50 feet.

224 **Facing Up (6)** ★   Obvious chimney left of *Hitchhiker*. Climb chimney all the way to the top. 50 feet.

225 **Eminent Front (10+)** ★★★★   Located forty feet right of *Albino Rhino*. Thin fingercrack (5.9) leads thirty feet up to a short roof. Go straight up and over the roof on smooth handholds. On the first ascent of this climb, the leader fell on an innocent bystander causing no injury but that of a rude awakening and a bruised ego. The leader then talked Greg Thomas into doing the lead, which Greg easily finished. Protection is tricky low on the route. At the roof, a two-to-three-inch horizontal crack makes great protection for cam devices. Protection above the roof is thin at best, so protect the roof well and be ready to run it out. This might be a good chance to see if that expensive equipment really does work. 55 feet. FFA: Craig Thomas/Keith Smith 1988.

226 **Overpowered by Funk (10+)** ★★★   Located ten feet left of *Eminent Front*. Arête on left end of wall. Boulder up to first bolt (5.10+) and past. Continue straight up past second bolt, mixed route. 65 feet. FFA: Woody Delp/Clay Frisbie 1991.

227 **Young Buzz (9)** ★★   Thin crack located five feet right of *Past the Jugs*. Start behind a tree on a thin crack moving right. At the ledge, come back a little to wide crack with bush in it and finish on jugs to the top (watch for loose rock). A little runout at the bottom. 50 feet. FFA: Woody Delp 4/91.

228 **Past the Jugs (10)** ★★★   A bolt is located three-quarters of the way up the face. Climb straight up the brown face (5.9) to the ledge. After bolt, reach high and to the right for a crack pocket; then move back left and up to top out. Sporty run out on 5.8+ climbing above bolt and 1.5 tri-cam. 50 feet. FFA: Gordon Callahan 1989.

229 **Chicken House (9+ TR)** ★★   Face between *Past the Jugs* and *Albino Rhino*. Boulder problem start. FFA: Andy Ash/Sean Burns 1992.

230 **Albino Rhino (7+)** ★★★★   If you find this obvious crack, you can find a number of other climbs. It is named after the horn located halfway up the route. If you can't find it, just ask; somebody will know. Obvious crack in a left-facing corner. This route is a good place to learn how to using stemming technique. The crux is the start of the route. This classic climb is one of the most popular lead routes on The Throne. 55 feet.

FEAR WALL

231   **Rocket Pocket (9 PG) ★★★★**   Located eight feet left of *Albino Rhino*. The first thirty-five feet of this route is superb face climbing. Start by dynoing for pocket or by making thin face move to reach pocket (5.9+). Continue above pocket by making 5.8+ face moves on pencil size edges. Pro for the first thirty-five feet is runout and some of the rest of the pro above is questionable. The climbing above is moderate (5.7). 70 feet.

232   **Free Blast (11)**   Same start as *Rocket Pocket*. This route is a very contrived variation of *Rocket Pocket*. On *Rocket Pocket* a little past the halfway point, climb straight up to the bolt and left. Take the path of most resistance climbing straight above the bolt. 70 feet.

233   **Face of Fear (10+ PG) ★★★**   Located five feet right of *Edge of Flight*. This climb might best be considered a boulder problem because the first twenty feet of the climb is the crux and protection does not avail itself until after the crux. The route then finishes the remaining part of *Edge of Flight*. Protection same as *Edge of Flight*. 80 feet. FFA: Billy Bisswanger 1989.

234   **Edge of Flight (10+ PG) ★★★★**   Perfect arête left of *Albino Rhino*. An Arkansas classic. This is a spectacular route that goes directly up the arête. The first twenty feet should be considered a boulder problem since protection does not avail itself. The crux, which is the first twenty feet, consists of pinches and balance moves. The remainder of the route is 5.8+ jug bashing up the arête. This route has seen several leads but seems to be a classic top-rope. Protection: No pro at the bottom and long runouts on looped horns above. 80 feet. FFA: Jim Karpowitz 1986.

PATIO WALL

235   **Dreadlock Rasta (A2+) ★★★★**   First ten feet is the same start as *Instant Karma*; then veer right following the thin crack line around the roof and up the steep face. This is the thin line that ascends what many call Plaque Wall. This is an exciting aid line that requires apt ability to nail. Please leave the two RURPs near the top fixed, because pulling them may destroy the placement. Also, take care not to overdrive pins because this too could destroy crucial placements. The plaque at the top of the wall is dedicated to Clint Karator, an avid climber who spent an abundance of time climbing in this area. Clint passed away in 1989 in an unfortunate automobile accident. Rack: 4 KBs, 6 LAs, 6 BAs, 1 RURP or birdbeak, possible 1 hook and standard rack. FA: Pat Meek

236   **Instant Karma (10+) ★★★★**   Crack located between *Patio Direct* and *Edge of Flight*. Start from ledge, climb up twenty feet on

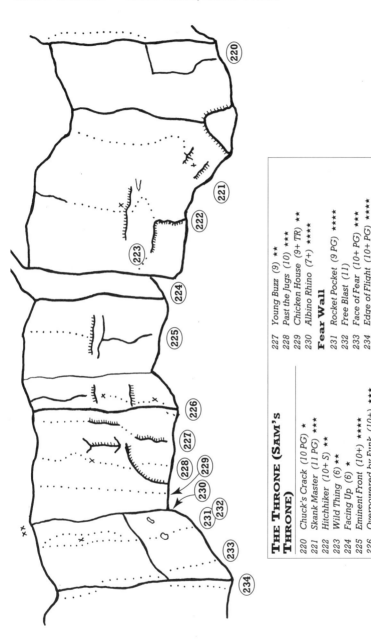

THE THRONE (SAM'S THRONE)

220 Chuck's Crack (10 PG) ★
221 Skank Master (11 PG) ★★★
222 Hitchhiker (10+ S) ★★
223 Wild Thing (6) ★★
224 Facing Up (6) ★
225 Eminent Front (10+) ★★★★
226 Overpowered by Funk (10+) ★★★

227 Young Buzz (9) ★★
228 Past the Jugs (10) ★★★
229 Chicken House (9+ TR) ★★
230 Albino Rhino (7+) ★★★★

Fear Wall

231 Rocket Pocket (9 PG) ★★★★
232 Free Blast (11)
233 Face of Fear (10+ PG) ★★★
234 Edge of Flight (10+ PG) ★★★★

orange rock to where the left-slanting crack begins. Climb smooth finger-hand crack (5.10+) fifteen feet to where it intersects with *Patio Direct*. Do a comfortable belay from this ledge. From here you can finish on *Patio Direct* or 3rd class sideways to the left. Note: This climb might be considered harder than 5.10+ if you are short or do not have arms that hang down to your feet. But I might be considered a little bit biased, because this is my best excuse for explaining my lack of ability to climb this. 40 feet. FFA: Jim Karpowitz 1986.

237 **Patio Direct (9 PG)** ★★★★ Corner left of the *Edge of Flight* on *Patio Wall*. Climb crack a few feet left of the corner (5.8 enjoyable) to large ledge with a roof. Turn right side of the roof (5.9) and continue up. Sporty runout after roof. Two-bolt top-rope anchor. 65 feet.

238 **Doing the Ritz (7)** ★★★ Located twenty feet left of *Patio Direct*, this superb route provides an excellent variety of sustained 5.6 and 5.7 moves. Start on a right-angling fifteen-foot crack up to a ledge. At the ledge, move left a few feet to a thin discontinuous crack. Ascend the crack line using face moves to the top. 55 feet.

THRONE PROPER

239 **To Lichen or not to Lichen (7)** ★★ Start on the left side of the low angle. Climb up and to the right using horizontal cracks for protection. 40 feet.

240 **Hamburger Helper (9)** ★★★★ Located on front side of Throne Proper next to the walkup. Thin crack that runs up and through a small roof. Pull the roof (5.9) and finish on chickenheads. 30 feet.

241 **Unknown (5th class)** Middle of the wall facing Blind Man's Bluff, climb path of least resistance to the top of Throne Proper. This is the easiest descent off Throne Proper. Another method to get off the Throne is to jump across using the cedar tree. 35 feet.

242 **Sonya, Tonya. What's the Difference? (7)** ★★★★ Thin crack that runs up the back side of Throne Proper. This popular route is extremely enjoyable but tricky to protect the angling, flared seam. 50 feet.

243 **Cinnamon (10)** ★★ Thirty feet right of *Sonya, Tonya*, around the corner with one bolt. 50 feet. FFA: Mark Bickford/Billy Bisswanger 1994.

BLIND MAN'S BLUFF

244 **Bloody Bowels (10 S)** ★★ Face climb just to the right of *Bloody Knuckles* with a two-inch horizontal crack located halfway up the

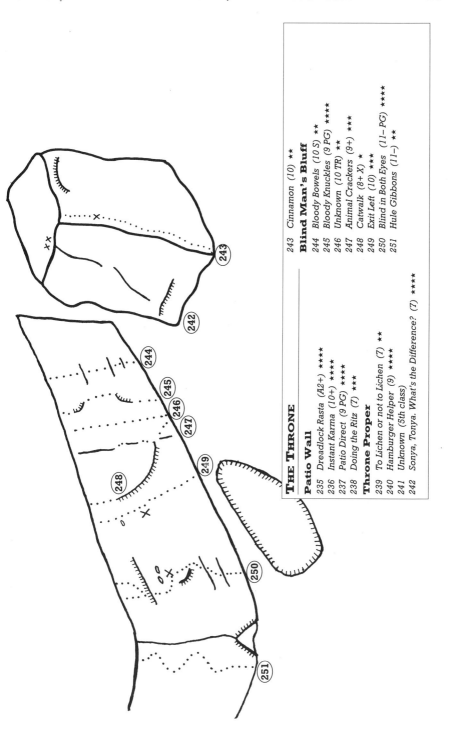

The Throne

Patio Wall

235 Dreadlock Rasta (A2+) ★★★★
236 Instant Karma (10+) ★★★★
237 Patio Direct (9 PG) ★★★★
238 Doing the Ritz (7) ★★★

Throne Proper

239 To Lichen or not to Lichen (7) ★★
240 Hamburger Helper (9) ★★★★
241 Unknown (5th class)
242 Sonya, Tonya, What's the Difference? (7) ★★★★

243 Cinnamon (10) ★★

Blind Man's Bluff

244 Bloody Bowels (10 S) ★★
245 Bloody Knuckles (9 PG) ★★★★
246 Unknown (10 TR) ★★
247 Animal Crackers (9+) ★★★
248 Catwalk (8+ X) ★
249 Exit Left (10) ★★★
250 Blind in Both Eyes (11– PG) ★★★★
251 Hule Gibbons (11–) ★★

route. Tricky to protect start of the route where the first crux move is. 50 feet. FFA: Frisbie/Hancock/Davidson/T. Karpowitz 1991.

245 **Bloody Knuckles (9 PG)** ★★★★ Located twenty feet left of throne walkdown on Blind Man's Bluff. This is the second route on this wall. Climb discontinuous thin crack. Protection is tricky the first twenty feet. 45 feet.

246 **Unknown (10 TR)** ★★ Face climb between *Animal Crackers* and *Bloody Knuckles*. 50 feet.

247 **Animal Crackers (9+)** ★★★ Thin crack that cuts through the base of the ramp dihedral. Boulder up fifteen feet to where thin crack begins and continue straight up climb. 60 feet.

248 **Catwalk (8+ X)** ★ Start in the middle of the wall on the right-facing ramp dihedral. Continue moving left up the ramp to the top. Length, if you count moving sideways, is 70 feet.

249 **Exit Left (10)** ★★★ Fifteen feet right of *Blind in Both Eyes* bolt located three-quarters the way up. Straight up thin chickenheads thirty-five feet (5.9). Reach for pocket above and to the left of the bolt (5.10). After that, reach for pocket up and to the right. Pull up and finish the climb from there. This move is harder on lead because the pocket you are putting your hand into is also the best place for pro. This route is a classic challenge for the would-be hardman! Protection: A 1.5 Tri Cam (red) for the pocket ten feet above bolt. 50 feet. FFA: Frisbie/Von Canon/Foster 1989.

250 **Blind in Both Eyes (11–PG)** ★★★★ Last route left on Blind Man's Bluff to the right of the arête on the bluff. Start climb fifteen feet right of the edge of the bluff on a sugary face (5.9). An exposed, strange, mantel-type move (5.9) is made before clipping the bolt. At the bolt, reach high and left using sloping holds (5.11–). Top out using sloping holds. This testpiece route was the start of a new wave of routes at Sam's Throne. Also, it was the first bolt to be placed at Sam's. Protection is a little tricky before reaching the bolt. 60 feet. FFA: Billy Bisswanger/Keith Smith 1987.

251 **Hule Gibbons (11–)** ★★ Arête face right of large tree left of *Blind in Both Eyes*. Good TR or sling tree branches for lead. 65 feet. FFA: Davidson/Tom Karpowitz/Stites 1991.

252 **Place in the Past (9)** ★ Thin crack twenty feet right of *Too Thick to Navigate*. Just right of a large tree coinciding with the bluff is a thin crack. Climb fifteen feet up to the crack (5.9). Continue with the crack system (5.9) to the top which ends with very moderate climbing. 50 feet. Protection: If you are hard up, the tree could hold a sling.

Billy Bisswanger on Blind in Both Eyes (11– PG) ★★★★, Blind Man's Bluff. Photo: Billy Bisswanger Collection.

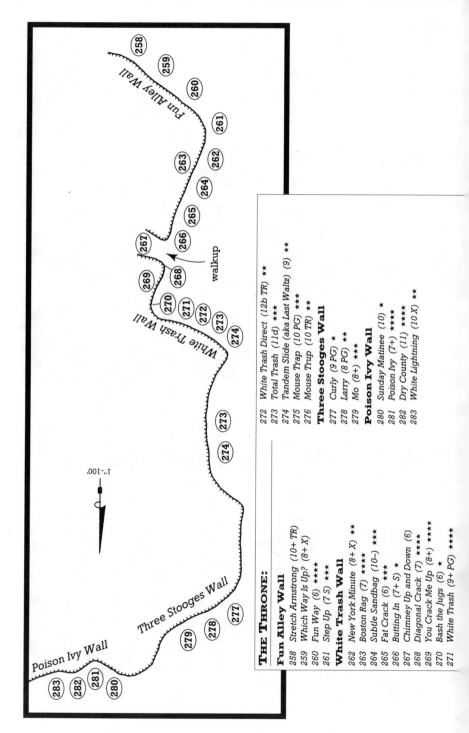

THE THRONE:

Fun Alley Wall

258 Stretch Armstrong (10+ TR)
259 Which Way Is Up? (8+ X)
260 Fun Way (6) ★★★★
261 Step Up (7 S) ★★★

White Trash Wall

262 New York Minute (8+ X) ★★
263 Boston Rag (7) ★★★★
264 Subtle Sandbag (10–) ★★★
265 Fat Crack (6) ★★★
266 Butting In (7+ S) ★
267 Chimney Up and Down (6)
268 Diagonal Crack (7) ★★★★
269 You Crack Me Up (8+) ★★★★
270 Bash the Jugs (6) ★
271 White Trash (9+ PG) ★★★★
272 White Trash Direct (12b TR) ★★
273 Total Trash (11d) ★★★
274 Tandem Slide (aka Last Waltz) (9) ★★
275 Mouse Trap (10 PG) ★★★
276 Mouse Trip (10 TR) ★★

Three Stooges Wall

277 Curly (9 PG) ★
278 Larry (8 PG) ★★
279 Mo (8+) ★★★

Poison Ivy Wall

280 Sunday Matinee (10) ★
281 Poison Ivy (7+) ★★★★
282 Dry County (11) ★★★★
283 White Lightning (10 X) ★★

253   **Too Thick to Navigate (8+) ★★★**   Large hand and fist jam crack. Crux is starting the route. 35 feet.

254   **Eating Peaches (7) ★**   Face between *Too Thick to Navigate* and *Dumbo's Crack*. FFA: Travis Carr.

255   **Dumbo's Crack (6)**   Wide dihedral crack with large death boulder balanced at the top of the dihedral. 40 feet.

256   **Mike's Crack (10–) ★★★★**   Prominent thin crack line in middle of face. Climb up sugary face twenty feet to a thin crack; continue in crack to the top. TCUs and nuts helpful. 50 feet. FFA: Jim Karpowitz 1986.

257   **Fur Piece (10 S) ★★**   Ten feet left of *Mike's Crack*. Straight up face/crack, reachy crux. Continue on moderate climbing. About a third of the way up, reach up left to a letter-box pocket then up and back right to the crack. FFA: Billy Bisswanger/Mark Bickford/Curtis Presley 1989.

FUN ALLEY WALL

258   **Stretch Armstrong (10+ TR)**   Right edge of Fun Alley Wall and left of *Mike's Crack*. Start just left of the edge. Make reachy moves to pull the roof at the top of the route. 50 feet.

259   **Which Way Is Up? (8+ X)**   Fifteen feet right of *Fun Way* on Fun Alley Wall. Straight up to roof and move left (5.6); continue up to blank section three-quarters the way up (5.8+). 60 feet.

260   **Fun Way (6) ★★★★**   Jug blast vertical wall up the path of least resistance. This route is just like climbing a ladder. Excellent route for beginners to find out what it is like to climb without having to look for the hand holds. By the way, one of the earlier ascents of this climb was done in the nude. Two bolt anchor. 60 feet.

261   **Step Up (7 S) ★★★**   Ascend arête left on Fun Alley Wall, thin pro. 60 feet.

WHITE TRASH WALL

262   **New York Minute (8+ X) ★★**   Face climb ten feet right of *Boston Rag*. Face climb straight up face with orange spot located about halfway up, staying just left of the arête. Protection very slim to none. 55 feet.

263   **Boston Rag (7) ★★★★**   Obvious handcrack that goes up the middle of the face. Begins with superb handcrack that narrows to a fingercrack. Then continue straight up and finish on chickenheads. This is a classic route. 60 feet.

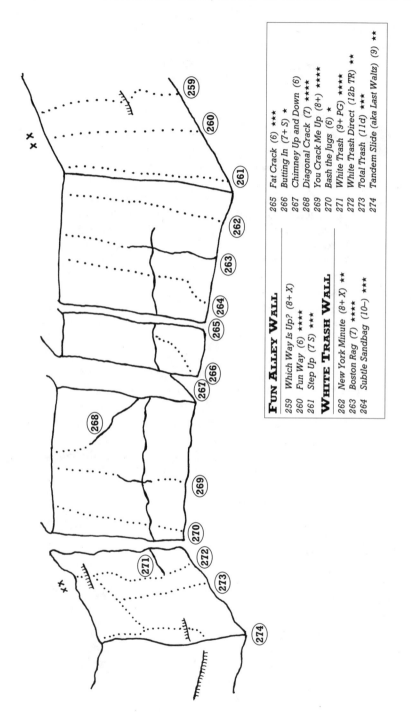

FUN ALLEY WALL

259 Which Way Is Up? (8+ X)
260 Fun Way (6) ★★★★
261 Step Up (7 S) ★★★

WHITE TRASH WALL

262 New York Minute (8+ X) ★★
263 Boston Rag (7) ★★★★
264 Subtle Sandbag (10−) ★★★

265 Fat Crack (6) ★★★
266 Butting In (7+ S) ★
267 Chimney Up and Down (6)
268 Diagonal Crack (7) ★★★★
269 You Crack Me Up (8+) ★★★★
270 Bash the Jugs (6) ★
271 White Trash (9+ PG) ★★★★
272 White Trash Direct (12b TR) ★★
273 Total Trash (11d) ★★★
274 Tandem Slide (aka Last Waltz) (9) ★★

264   **Subtle Sandbag (10–) ★★★**   Face located between *Fat Crack* and *Boston Rag*. Start with finger pocket located seven feet off the ground. Boulder up and to the right using friction holds (5.10) for fifteen feet, then blast to the top on chickenheads (5.6). As you might guess, this was a favored place to sandbag other climbers unfamiliar with the climb if it can be called that. A one-move wonder. 45 feet. Protection: Boulder problem

265   **Fat Crack (6) ★★★**   Climb the wide crack. 45 feet.

266   **Butting In (7+ S) ★**   From the right edge of the corner, move right and up using friction and smooth holds (5.7+). After the vertical crack, join *Fat Crack* (5.6). No pro at start of route. 45 feet.

267   **Chimney Up and Down (6)**   Obvious chimney breaking up White Trash Wall. Climb inside the chimney at the outermost edge all the way to the top. To call this a real climb is probably a good joke, but it does get climbed. It is a good place to break a sweat and practice chimneying. Farther inside the chimney is an easy walkup. There is no real protection. 45 feet.

268   **Diagonal Crack (7) ★★★★**   Thin diagonal crack. Start on left corner of chimney walkdown. Climb up fifteen feet to where the diagonal crack begins, follow the crack moving left. 35 feet. FFA: Billy Bisswanger 1987.

269   **You Crack Me Up (8+) ★★★★**   Prominent thin crack in middle of face. Boulder up to thin crack finishing with, what else?, chickenheads. 45 feet. FFA: Jerry Cagle 1987.

270   **Bash the Jugs (6) ★**   Start on the right face of the diagonal corner. Continue straight up jugs. 45 feet.

271   **White Trash (9+ PG) ★★★★**   The orange wall that is left of White Trash Wall. Start up dihedral and do hand traverse left for twelve feet. From here, climb straight up face to the roof (5.9 PG). Top out by pulling roof (5.10). A heel hook might come in handy here. This route has been led several times but seems to be a top-rope classic. Two-bolt anchor. 50 feet.

272   **White Trash Direct (12b TR) ★★**   Direct start to *White Trash*. Go straight up, eliminating the traverse. 50 feet.

273   **Total Trash (11d) ★★★**   Face climb with thin holds between *Last Waltz* and *White Trash*. This route possibly has been lead, but I would recommend it as a top-rope because of the bleak protection at the crux. 50 feet.

274   **Tandem Slide (aka Last Waltz) (9) ★★**   Start in a weird crack in face, then climb the corner moving straight up and to the right. Top out on ledge or traverse right and finish on *White Trash* roof (5.10 S). 40 feet. FFA: Jerry Cagle/Keith Smith 1987.

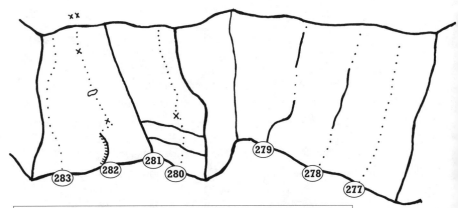

THREE STOOGES WALL	POISON IVY WALL
277 Curly (9 PG) ★ 278 Larry (8 PG) ★★ 279 Mo (8+) ★★★	280 Sunday Matinee (10) ★ 281 Poison Ivy (7+) ★★★★ 282 Dry County (11) ★★★★ 283 White Lightning (10 X) ★★

275   **Mouse Trap (10 PG)** ★★★   This route is located a couple hundred feet to the left around the corner from *Tandem Slide*. This route ascends the middle of the smooth, light green face. Climb up to small finger-size pocket. Climb above pocket to two ledges with horizontal cracks and finish climb by moving around roof system. Tricky to protect the crux move on the bottom section of the route. 60 feet. FFA: Delp/Frisbie/Eric Peterson 1990.

276   **Mouse Trup (10 TR)** ★★   Located left of *Mouse Trap*.

THREE STOOGES WALL

277   **Curly (9 PG)** ★   Ten feet right of *Larry*. Climb up face fifteen feet to discontinuous crack. Follow crack to a small roof; pull roof by using chickenheads. 50 feet.

278   **Larry (8 PG)** ★★   Ten feet right of *Mo*. Discontinuous crack, top out with jug bashing. 50 feet.

279   **Mo (8+)** ★★★   First crack to the right around corner from *Poison Ivy* on Three Stooges Wall. Climb straight up to large fist-size crack. Pull small roof and straight up. Large pro! 50 feet.

POISON IVY WALL

280   **Sunday Matinee (10)** ★   Route with bolt to the right of *Poison Ivy*. Climb straight up to the bolt; do crux move and continue up the route searching for the path of most resistance. 50 feet. FFA: Chip ? 1990.

281   **Poison Ivy (7+)** ★★★★   Where the trail forks at the throne, go to
the right fifty feet. An obvious dihedral handcrack on a low-angle
slab. This is one of the most striking cracks at Sam's. Follow the
crack all the way to the top. The crux is not to grab the dead
stump that is located six feet from the top. This classic route is
probably led more than any other route at Sam's Throne. Two-
bolt anchor on top. 55 feet. Protection: Great! If you can't protect
this route, you had better leave your rack at home!

282   **Dry County (11)** ★★★★   Two-bolt friction climb ten feet left of
Poison Ivy. Twenty feet of easy crack and face climbing leads to
first bolt. Go to the left and straight up with weird mantel (5.10). At
the top of the route, follow the scoop to the left of the second bolt
(5.11). Sorry! No chickenheads on this one. This route is one of
the very few friction climbs at Sam's. This is a great climb to do at
the end of the day when you don't have any forearm strength left.
This is probably one of the cheapest 5.11s because the rating
comes from one hard move located at the top of the route that
was made more difficult by a broken foothold. Also, a bolt is at
waist level when pulling the crux. Tri-cams 3 and 3.5 may come in
extremely handy for the pocket located between the two bolts. 55
feet. FFA: Stites/Davidson/T Karpowitz 1990.

283   **White Lightning (10 X)** ★★   Start left of the opening in the rock
that is left of *Dry County.* It is a friction climb with several balance
moves on sloping friction holds with little or no protection at crux
sections. This route should be considered more as a solo. This
route was first top-roped before it was lead. 55 feet. FFA: Dennis
Nelms.

Carmelita Angeles on Dry County (5.11)
★★★★, *Posion Ivy Wall. Photo: Billy
Bisswanger.*

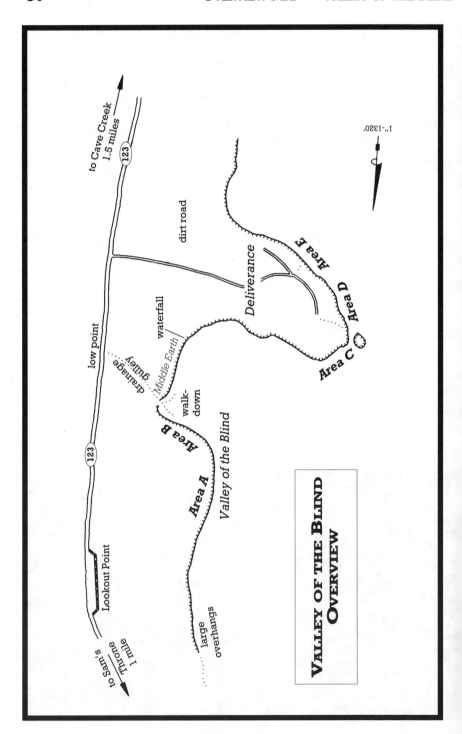

to Cave Creek
1.5 miles

123

1"-1320'.

dirt road

to Sam's
Throne
1 mile

123

Lookout Point

low point

drainage
gulley

Middle Earth

waterfall

walk-
down

Area B

Area A

Valley of the Blind

large
overhangs

Deliverance

Area E

Area D

Area C

**VALLEY OF THE BLIND
OVERVIEW**

CHAPTER THREE

VALLEY OF THE BLIND AND DELIVERANCE

Valley of the Blind, with its colorful walls, sports the tallest routes of the entire area, with many of the routes reaching one hundred feet. With a vast amount of high quality routes, adventure abounds with many of the routes being of a serious nature. With south-facing walls, the sun's warmth makes winter climbing a pleasant possibility. Valley of the Blind is located one-half mile downhill from the Lookout Point at the low point in the road just before going back up the next hill. Park along side of the road then follow the drainage system west downhill. It is a ten- to fifteen-minute hike into the valley.

1   **The Beholder (10)** ★★★   Located at the start of the massive roof system with rough grey rock is a handcrack which leads through a very large improbable roof that appears to be more difficult to climb than it actually is. 100 feet. FFA: Clay Frisbie/Tom Hancock 12/94.

1a   **Wisdom and Folly (11b/c)** ★★★★   South face of prominent orange protruding column. Climb up steep face past seven bolts on this dynamic route. This striking route is saturated with 5.10 climbing and one tricky undercling crux move to captivate your attention. Two-bolt anchor. 80 feet. FFA: Clay Frisbie/Barry Gilbert 2/97.

1b   **Deep & Wide (10–)** ★★★   Chimney that reduces to a offwidth near the top. An exceptional climb full of 5.8 chimney climbing to hone your chimneying technique. 75 feet. FFA: Clay Frisbie/Chandler Schooler.

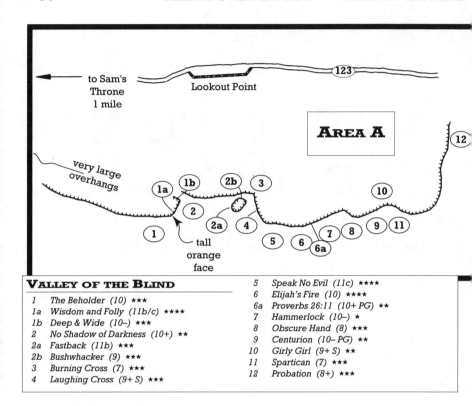

VALLEY OF THE BLIND

1	The Beholder (10) ★★★	
1a	Wisdom and Folly (11b/c) ★★★★	
1b	Deep & Wide (10–) ★★★	
2	No Shadow of Darkness (10+) ★★	
2a	Fastback (11b) ★★★	
2b	Bushwhacker (9) ★★★	
3	Burning Cross (7) ★★★	
4	Laughing Cross (9+ S) ★★★	

5	Speak No Evil (11c) ★★★★	
6	Elijah's Fire (10) ★★★★	
6a	Proverbs 26:11 (10+ PG) ★★	
7	Hammerlock (10–) ★	
8	Obscure Hand (8) ★★★	
9	Centurion (10– PG) ★★	
10	Girly Girl (9+ S) ★★	
11	Spartican (7) ★★★	
12	Probation (8+) ★★★	

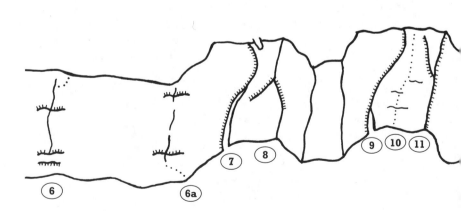

2   **No Shadow of Darkness (10+)** ★★   Start twenty feet right of offwidth dihedral. Climb up sloping white face through a watergroove (5.9 S) thirty feet up to a handcrack, then twenty feet to the top (5.10+). 75 feet. FFA: Clay Frisbie/Tom Hancock 12/94.

2a   **Fastback (11b)** ★★★   North face of protruding column of rock. Technical moves lead up this thought-provoking clean face past five bolts. A one-inch crack easily accepts needful protection near the top. Two-bolt anchor. 55 feet. FFA: Barry Gilbert/Clay Frisbie 2/97.

2b   **Bushwhacker (9)** ★★★   On south side of protruding column, stem up chimney to achieve crack system. Follow crack system for adventuresome and interesting route to the top. FFA: Tim Dement/Barry Gilbert 2/97.

3   **Burning Cross (7)** ★★★   Very sustained left-facing dihedral offwidth crack.

4   **Laughing Cross (9+ S)** ★★★   In the middle of less than vertical white face. A two-foot cross formed by a vertical and horizontal crack halfway up mark this unique climb. Climb up to cross then angle up and right through the middle of the face to the top. The only real protection is at the cross and the crux of the route. [On the first ascent Woody—over halfway up the face—fell while laughing about how the route did not need a bolt. In the process the fall ripped out his protection resulting in a grounder. Well it didn't get a bolt and Woody went back up and finished the route.] 85 feet. FFA: Woody Delp/Tom Hancock 1991.

5   **Speak No Evil (11c)** ★★★★   Start on the orange arête then move left (5.11) to ascend through roof (5.10). Then follow dihedral with tricky moves (5.11c) to the top exit right with an exciting hand traverse. Nine bolts with two-bolt anchor. 90 feet. FFA: Clay Frisbie/Tom Hancock/Bob Sheier 1997.

6   **Elijah's Fire (10)** ★★★★   Start in the obvious overhanging crack system by pulling up to ledge. Maneuver through a slot to an orange overhanging roof (5.9+) with a crack. Follow crack system to a thin crack (5.10) to top out. Read I Kings Chapter 18 if you want to know about the name. 80 feet. FFA: Clay Frisbie/Tom Hancock 1991.

6a   **Proverbs 26:11 (10+ PG)** ★★   Thin crack system that splits the orange rock buttress. 60 feet. FFA: Clay Frisbie/Tom Hancock 3/97.

7   **Hammerlock (10–)** ★   Right-angling offwidth crack. 50 feet. FFA: Clay Frisbie/Tim Childs 3/97.

8   **Obscure Hand (8)** ★★★   Perfect handcrack. 50 feet.

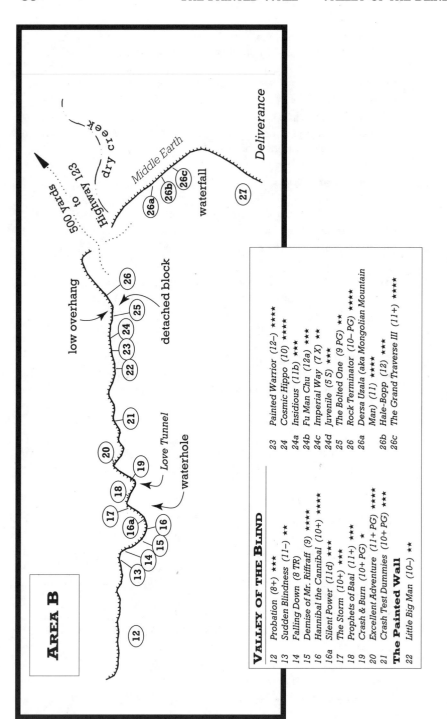

9   **Centurion (10– PG)** ★★   Right-angling crack system in orange rock. 50 feet. FFA: Clay Frisbie/Bob Sheier 3/93.

10 **Girly Girl (9+ S)** ★★   Climb middle of face between *Spartican* and *Centurion.* Small protection. 50 feet. FFA: Bob Sheier/Clay Frisbie 3/93.

11 **Spartican (7)** ★★★   Left-angling crack that ends with a chimney at the top. 50 feet. FFA: Bob Sheier 3/93.

12 **Probation (8+)** ★★★   Right-leaning diagonal crack leads to an offwidth at the top. 40 feet. FFA: Keary Allen 1992.

13 **Sudden Blindness (11–)** ★★   Moderate climbing leads to a tree growing out of a dirty crack. A short overhang leads to a right-facing finger dihedral crack (5.11–). 60 feet. FFA: Clay Frisbie/Keary Allen 1992.

14 **Falling Down (8 TR)**   Enjoyable face climb up orange rock between two crack systems.

15 **Demise of Mr. Riffraff (9)** ★★★★   Twenty feet of face climbing leads to an unmistakable handcrack. Thirty feet of sustained 5.9 crack climbing leads to a large tree near the top. 55 feet. FFA: Clay Frisbie/Mike Stites 1992.

16 **Hannibal the Cannibal (10+)** ★★★★   Start on orange rock face, climbing up twenty feet past one bolt to a conspicuous thin crack. Thin crack winds into a left-leaning overhanging handcrack. After crux near the top you can traverse right to a two-bolt anchor or top out. The quality of rock is much better than it looks. Bring lots of gear, this climb takes it all. 90 feet. FFA: Clay Frisbie/Tom Hancock 1991.

16a **Silent Power (11d)** ★★★   Crack system that leads up and under the large overhanging prow. **(P1)** Mixed route (5.10+) leads past four bolts to a bolted belay under prow. **(P2)** The first bolt maybe hard to spot (reach up and far left around arête). From the belay traverse left with delicate moves to achieve a stance around the corner(5.11). A pumpfest (5.11d) finish past two bolts to top out, traverse left to two-bolt anchor. 100 feet. FFA: Tony Mayse/Clay Frisbie 2/97.

17 **The Storm (10+)** ★★★   A large pool of sometime stagnate water resides just right of the start of this route. The route ascends an improbable looking roof. This roof is so large and overhanging that even during a raging storm, this route stayed completely dry except for the exit at the top. Start in the large offwidth crack, climb to a point where you can traverse left into the base of where the next crack system starts. Squirm and squeeze through the offwidth (5.10+) gaining access through the roof system. A long-

sleeve shirt and pants might help to preserve the epidermis, the rock is a bit abrasive! FFA: Clay Frisbie/Tom Hancock 7/94.

18   **Prophets of Baal (11+)** ★★★   Start just left of large tree. Climb twenty feet on dark-colored rock to first bolt. A second bolt leads through the first roof system and crux. The route then continues up orange rock and three more bolts lead to the second roof before topping out. The name of this route came from the first top-rope. [While top-roping this route for the first time and just finishing the last overhang, a fifty-pound block pulled off on my head, which besides ruining my first attempt at this route, raised a goose egg lump and also brought back the startling reality that climbing is always dangerous even when top-roping. (I Kings 18:40)]. 90 feet. FFA: Clay Frisbie/Tom Hancock 1992.

19   **Crash & Burn (10+ PG)** ★   Climbing thirty feet up a detached block leads to the start of a crack system that extends through a roof and straight up the orange face. Pass three bolts to maneuver through roof (5.10). Sustained 5.9+ climbing up the crack system leads past two more bolts beyond which lie several 5.10+ moves to top out. Mixed pro, tri-cams and cams for half-inch to one-and-a-half-inch crack. 90 feet. FFA: Frisbie/Caughlin/Hancock 1/95.

20   **Excellent Adventure (11+ PG)** ★★★★   Climb orange face past one bolt (5.11+) to a thin crack system that becomes larger as the route continues. The route ends with an exciting overhanging roof crack (5.11−). This is fascinating climbing on enticing rock. 100 feet. FFA: Clay Frisbie/Tom Hancock 1991.

21   **Crash Test Dummies (10+ PG)** ★★★   Winding crack system through orange face with first bolt located thirty feet up. Several captivating moves using both face and crack lead to the handcrack crux at the top. Although this route has four bolts, a wide range of protection is needed to properly protect this route because of rotten rock. 100 feet. FFA: Clay Frisbie/Chuck Caughlin 1/95.

THE PAINTED WALL

One morning while trying to climb at Deliverance, our climbing party found all the routes wet from seeping water. So, in search of dry south-facing rock on this winter day, we hiked across the valley. To our amazement what at first appeared to be short cliffs were ninety-foot cliffs with spectacular features. The first wall that we saw was Painted Warrior. Because of the spectacular colors of the wall and the perfect rock patio at its base, one could imagine that this surely must have been where Native Americans had sat years before enjoying the same beauty of this spot. It seemed obvious at the time that any ascent up this wall would be a striking line and extraordinary climb. All I can

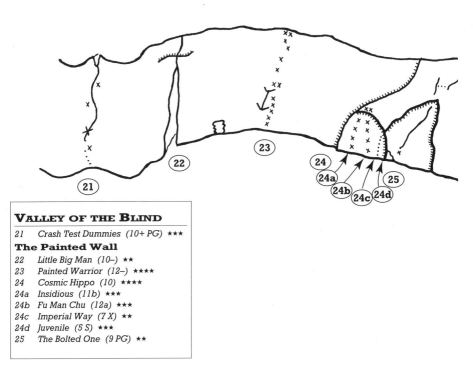

say is we were not disappointed when we climbed Painted Warrior one year later.

22   **Little Big Man (10–)** ★★   Chimney located on the left side of The Painted Wall. Intriguing chimney climbing (5.7) for fifty feet leads to an overhanging roof crack. This climb does protect better than it appears. 90 feet. FFA: Clay Frisbie/Tom Hancock 1991.

23   **Painted Warrior (12–)** ★★★★   This line ascends the middle of The Painted Wall with ten bolts for protection. With four crux sections and ninety feet of sustained climbing, this route is a prized red point. Inspiration for this route was born one year before it was ever climbed. Ten bolts and a two-bolt anchor. 90 feet. FFA: Frisbie/Hancock/Ken Oeser 1992.

24   **Cosmic Hippo (10)** ★★★★   This route is generally wet during the winter and spring from water soaking down through the crack system, but when dry it is a reward for those seeking good crack and offwidth climbing. Located on the right side of The Painted Wall, this route starts in the left-facing dihedral handcrack (5.9) that leads up forty feet to a large ledge with a tree. This spot would make an excellent place to set up a belay for those wishing

Bob Scheier working his way past the plaque on Dreadlock Rasta (A2+) ★★★★, The Throne, Patio Wall. Photo: Ladd Campbell.

to do the route in two pitches. Continue in the crack system to the roof. Several opposition moves through the offwidth lead to the top. A large, six- to seven-inch cam might help relieve a little stress when protecting the top portion of this route. With several opposition moves and spectacular stances, this route is superb for aspiring crack and offwidth climbers. FFA: Tom Hancock/Clay Frisbie 7/94.

24a   Insidious (11b) ★★★   Delicate moves on brown streak lead up past four bolts, two-bolt anchor. 45 feet. FFA: Clay Frisbie/Jackie Allard/Tim Childs 3/97.

24b   Fu Man Chu (12a) ★★★   Sustained delicate moves lead up past four bolts, two-bolt anchor. 45 feet. FFA: Clay Frisbie/Jackie Allard/Tim Childs 3/97.

24c   Imperial Way (7 X) ★★   Arête on right side of boulder. Boulder up right side following the arête to the top of the boulder. 45 feet.

24d   Juvenile (5 S) ★★★   South side of boulder, climb up middle of less than vertical face. 45 feet.

25   The Bolted One (9 PG) ★★   Start on a face which is actually an enormous detached flake that is thirty-five-feet high. Face climb past one bolt to a thin crack which leads up to a large ledge on the top of the flake. Second pitch starts in the left crack (rotten rock), then traverses into the more defined crack on the right to top out. This route can be done in one or two pitches. *The Bolted One* was the first bolt placed in the entire Sam's Throne Area. Around the mid-'80s Billy Bisswanger and Craig Thomas originally came down into Valley of the Blind. They spied the bolt and climbed the route reporting the unique climbing and tall walls the area had to offer. It is still a mystery who placed the bolt and when. 85 feet.

26   Rock Terminator (10– PG) ★★★★   Boulder fifteen feet (5.9+) up onto a large ledge on the right side. Walk left to where the crack starts then climb the crack for enjoyable 5.8 climbing with the crux at the top. Take large pro, it may come in handy. 100 feet. FFA: Clay Frisbie/Pat Murphy 3/92.

26a   Dersa Uzala (aka Mongolian Mountain Man) (11) ★★★★
Black stain on the lower potion of this route with four bolts is the most obvious feature. This route has it all—technical face climbing, crack climbing, steep rock and offwidth. Bring a wide selection of gear. This spectacular route is just at one hundred feet. FFA: Clay Frisbie/Tom Hancock 3/97.

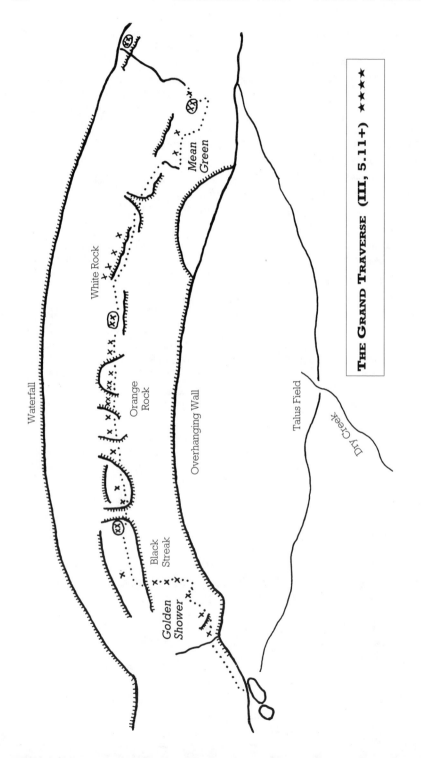

26b   **Hale-Bopp (12)** ★★★   A crack system that runs through three separate roofs. Start at the orange overhang (5.11) that leads up steep rock past two bolts into the crack system on the left. At the next roof one bolt leads to finger-hand crack above and through overhang (5.10). At the last roof powerful awkward moves (5.12) lead past two bolts to the top. Two-bolt anchor. 100 feet. FFA: Clay Frisbie/Chandler Schooler 4/97.

26c   **The Grand Traverse (III, 11+)** ★★★★   This route traverses under the overhanging waterfall (seasonal) and above the prominent one hundred-foot overhang that drops off below. This unbelievable route follows the weakness along the middle of the face. Possibly the longest route in the Midwest, this five-hundred-foot route is made up of three traversing pitches of 5.10-5.11 and one vertical pitch of 5.11 that takes you to the top. This spectacular route is a one of a kind, with the unmistakable feel of the "big wall" as the ground drops off at the start of the route. **(P1)** "The Golden Shower." Step onto the wall from a protruding boulder traverse right to first bolt then move up and right. This section is wet during the spring but climbable, enjoy the light shower. Continue moving up and right past two more bolts (5.10). At the black vertical streak climb past four bolts (5.10) with one move of 5.11+. 150 feet, two-bolt belay. **(P2)** Traverse right past twelve bolts and several interesting moves(5.10+), 150 feet. **(P3)** "Mean Green." Traverse right past four bolts (5.9) along the face, moving downward at the overhang. Transverse right under the overhang past two bolts along thought-provoking green slab (5.10), two-bolt hanging belay, 120 feet. **(P4)** Move past one bolt (5.11) to obtain crack system. Follow crack system through overhang (5.11–), two-bolt rap anchor at stance above the roof or top out completely (seasonally wet) exit to the left. Awkward belay, 80 feet. FFA: Clay Frisbie/Chandler Schooler 2nd, 3rd, 4th pitch 3/97. Clay Frisbie/Tim Childs/Jackie Allard 1st pitch 3/97.

DELIVERANCE

Deliverance can be seen from Sam's Throne from atop Patio Wall. It is the tall north-facing bluff line across the valley. This area retains numerous ideal finger, fist and hand cracks. During the spring and winter this area is prone to water seepage making some of the rock wet. The best climbing conditions are during the summer and fall.

This area is must be approached from Valley of the Blind to avoid crossing private property. Do not approach Deliverance from on top unless you have specific permission to do so! The top of Deliverance lies mostly on private property. There is no camping or driving past the gate. This is private land, please respect it as such.

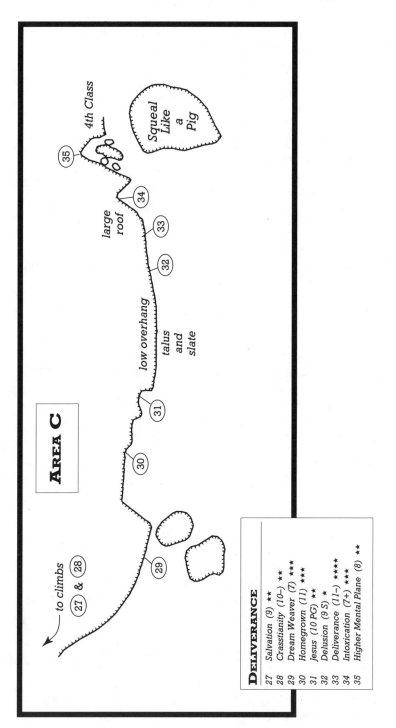

Area C

to climbs
27 & 28

4th Class

Squeal Like a Pig

large roof

low overhang

talus and slate

35
34
33
32
31
30
29

Deliverance

27   Salvation (9) ★★
28   Crasstianity (10−) ★★
29   Dream Weaver (7) ★★★
30   Homegrown (11) ★★★
31   Jesus (10 PG) ★★
32   Delusion (9 S) ★
33   Deliverance (11−) ★★★★
34   Intoxication (7+) ★★★
35   Higher Mental Plane (8) ★★

27   **Salvation (9)** ★★   Uphill from the base of a periodic one-hundred-foot waterfall. Climb the left-arching, overhanging handcrack. 35 feet. FFA: Clay Frisbie/Mike Stites 1/92.

28   **Crasstianity (10–)** ★★   Face and crack. 50 feet. FFA: Mike Stites/Clay Frisbie 1/92.

29   **Dream Weaver (7)** ★★★   Perfect handcrack on a low-angle wall with a small roof to top out. Not much more to say about this route other than enjoy. 35 feet.

30   **Homegrown (11)** ★★★   A distinct thin crack with intermittent handjams in a left-facing dihedral with light colored walls. Thirty-five feet of interesting, sustained climbing requiring great handjams, finger locks and precise footwork lead to a ledge. Twenty feet of moderate climbing up the remaining crack system leads to the top. As a drainage spot for the bluff line, this route normally has a light covering of dirt which makes climbing more difficult. If not for the dirt, this route would be a classic 5.10; but more than likely this route will always have a nice slick dusting. Even with the dirt this route is well worth climbing. FFA: Clay Frisbie/Mike Stites 1992.

31   **Jesus (10 PG)** ★★   A thin crack in a left-facing dihedral that widens to a noticeable six-inch crack on black rock. 40 feet. FFA: Chuck Caughlin/Clay Frisbie 10/94.

32   **Delusion (9 S)** ★   Start in overhanging, dirty offwidth. Bouldery ten feet leads to an overhanging roof crack. After the roof, follow mossy crack, that is more difficult than would appear, thirty feet to the bench-sized ledge that horizontally bisects the entire northwest face. At the ledge several options are available to finish the route. Many possible crack systems lead to the top. The crack system to the right provides interesting 5.9 climbing on solid rock. 50 feet. FFA: Clay Frisbie/Chuck Caughlin 10/94.

33   **Deliverance (11–)** ★★★★   This area holds a spectacular view of the Sam's Throne area. From here one can see everything from Northern Exposure to Valley of the Blind. Not only is this one of the best routes at Deliverance, but with such a view, belaying ain't so bad either. Begin the first pitch with a forty-foot handcrack on slightly mossy white rock (5.10) up to a spacious ledge with a tree to set up a comfortable belay. On a hot day the cool breeze that pours out of the crack on the first pitch is quite a relief. The second pitch ascends the obvious left-leaning, overhanging, large crack that leads to the top (5.11–). On the second pitch, placing protection is strenuous but a no-hands leglock can be found halfway up in a large horizontal crack. (Of course, being able to

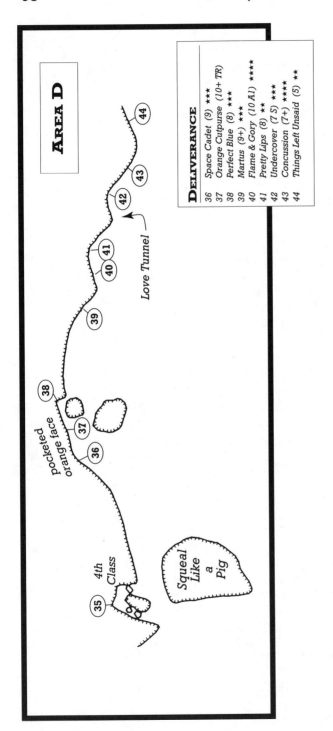

Area D

4th Class

pocketed
orange face

Love Tunnel

Squeal
Like
a
Pig

Deliverance

36 Space Cadet (9) ★★★
37 Orange Cutpurse (10+ TR)
38 Perfect Blue (8) ★★★
39 Martus (9+) ★★★
40 Flame & Gory (10 A1) ★★★★
41 Pretty Lips (8) ★★
42 Undercover (7.5) ★★★
43 Concussion (7+) ★★★★
44 Things Left Unsaid (5) ★★

achieve a no-hands rest is a 50% probability. The real question is "do you feel lucky?") Also, a chockstone at the top of the route can be lassoed with a couple of large runners to help relieve tension when topping out. 100 feet. FFA: Clay Frisbie/Mike Stites 1992.

34 **Intoxication (7+)** ★★★ Right-facing dihedral crack in slightly mossy white rock. One side of the dihedral is less than vertical. The top of the route is capped by an extensive roof system. Rap down at the fixed sling. 40 feet. FFA: Sean Burns/Amy Calvert 1994.

35 **Higher Mental Plane (8)** ★★ Dihedral crack located behind two large boulders, one of which is leaning against the wall. Climb under or through the boulder to approach the start of the route. Start in left-facing dihedral handcrack. FFA: Chuck Caughlin 10/94.

36 **Space Cadet (9)** ★★★ Left of *Orange Cutpurse* is a right-facing thin dihedral crack system on grey colored rock that leads to a large ledge. Continue with a right-facing dihedral crack system straight up through the roof. An excellent natural line that provides the easiest way up this section of steep wall. 85 feet. FFA: Clay Frisbie/Tom Hancock 1991.

37 **Orange Cutpurse (10+ TR)** Face on orange rock with pockets.

38 **Perfect Blue (8)** ★★★ Dihedral handcrack located back inside corridor. This route is short but very sweet. 35 feet.

39 **Martus (9+)** ★★★ Conspicuous classic handcrack on white colored rock that passes through two roofs. Crack ends on large ledge. Continue straight up twenty more feet on jugs. 80 feet. FFA: Clay Frisbie/Tom Hancock 1991.

40 **Flame & Gory (10 A1)** ★★★★ Just left of left-facing dihedral, a very outstanding handcrack splits an orange face. Forty feet of 5.9 climbing lead to a pronounced, jutting flake where the crack widens to a fistcrack and things get more interesting (5.10 weird!). At this point, the fifty-foot vertical crack is capped by an extensive overhang, and several options are available: 1) traverse right on direct aid (A1) past a fixed pin. This is the way the route was originally done and makes for some meritorious adventure; 2) free climb (5.11) the traverse which usually has a wet spot and is hard to protect; 3) the most lenient option is to rap from the sport rap anchors located at the top of the crack just under the roof. If you choose adventure (option one or two), the belay is best at the corner of the roof after the traverse. This will help cut down on rope drag. Bring extra big cams; they may come in handy on the fistcrack. 50–85 feet. FFA: Billy Bisswanger 1990.

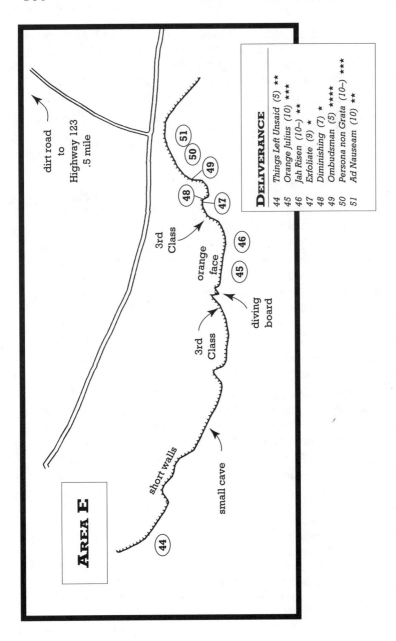

Area E

dirt road
to
Highway 123
.5 mile

3rd
Class

orange
face

3rd
Class

diving
board

short walls

small cave

Deliverance

44　Things Left Unsaid (5) ★★
45　Orange Julius (10) ★★★
46　Jah Risen (10–) ★★
47　Exfoliate (9) ★
48　Diminishing (7) ★
49　Ombudsman (5) ★★★★
50　Persona non Grata (10–) ★★★
51　Ad Nauseam (10) ★★

41   Pretty Lips (8) ★★   Dihedral crack. Chimney up twenty feet (5.6) to a handcrack. Same finish as *Flame & Gory* exit to the right under large roof. 80 feet.

42   Undercover (7 S) ★★★   Offwidth crack right of tunnel. First half of offwidth is hard to protect, but the second half of the route is a handcrack. 75 feet.

43   Concussion (7+) ★★★★   This route is bound to be a classic with good hand holds that line the entire crack system making this route very congenial and much easier than it would appear. Start in slightly overhanging handcrack , then straight up the thin crack line on the orange face. When crack ends, traverse left into the large crack system to top out. 75 feet.

44   Things Left Unsaid (5) ★★   Flaring chimney offwidth up less than vertical surface. 60 feet.

45   Orange Julius (10) ★★★   Prominent handcrack line that runs up middle of slightly overhanging orange face through two roofs. At ledge at top, traverse up and right through large blocks to good trees for your belay. 80 feet. FFA: Clay Frisbie/Tom Hancock 1991.

46   Jah Risen (10–) ★★   A handcrack , just right of tree, on dark colored rock. The crack runs through two roofs. 60 feet. FFA: Roderick Franklin/Clay Frisbie 5/94.

47   Exfoliate (9) ★   Large right-arching flake that starts as an offwidth then narrows first to fist and then a handcrack. Top out to the left on large ledge at Ombudsman. 45 feet.

48   Diminishing (7) ★   Large offwidth dihedral crack. Tops out at *Ombudsman* on large ledge. 45 feet.

49   Ombudsman (5) ★★★★   Large dihedral crack right of *Persona non Grata*. A long crack system up a vertical wall with good hand holds and protection spaced throughout make for a classic moderate route. 65 feet. FFA: Chuck Caughlin 7/94.

50   Persona non Grata (10–) ★★★   A thin crack runs through orange face past two pitons and two bolts. Above second bolt traverse left to top out at the large fistcrack. A rappel anchor is located on top of ledge. 70 feet. FFA: Frisbie/Caughlin/Hancock 7/94.

51   Ad Nauseam (10) ★★   Ten feet right of *Persona non Grata,* mount face to thin discontinuous crack. Continue straight up face, thin placements. At large ledge walk off or finish with easy climbing to the left. Belay straight above from a large tree. 70 feet. FFA: Clay Frisbie/Tom Hancock 1991.

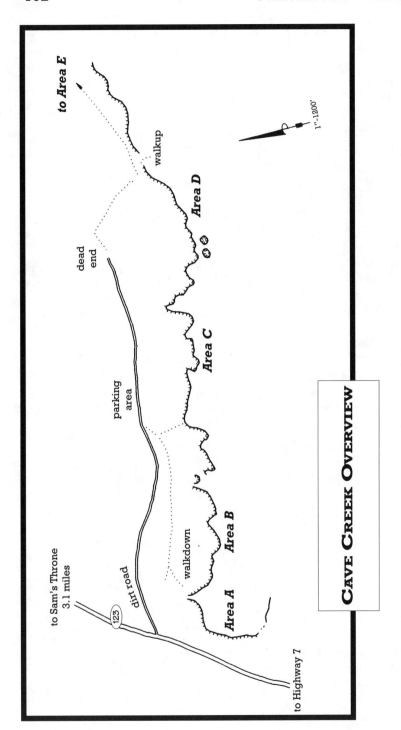

CAVE CREEK OVERVIEW

to Area E

walkup

Area D

dead
end

Area C

parking
area

1"=1200'

walkdown

Area B

dirt road

Area A

to Sam's Throne
3.1 miles

123

to Highway 7

CHAPTER FOUR

CAVE CREEK

Cave Creek is located 3.4 miles south of Sam's Throne along Highway 123. Take an old logging road that is on the east side of Highway 123. Follow dirt road for a quarter mile through a perpetual mud puddle to a clearing. A trail leads off to the south. From here it is an easy ten-minute approach into the valley. Good quality rock and an easy approach has led to the quick development and popularity of this area. A large number of routes are bolt-protected clip-ups(sport routes). There are also some exceptional mixed pro and traditional routes. This area with south-facing bluffs offers good climbing year round. With ratings a bit on the lenient side, climbing here may afford a boost in self confidence. Starting in 1989 Woody Delp, Chuck Foster and Mike Giner ventured into the pristine canyon setting of Cave Creek. They immediately discovered the excellent climbing possibilities of Cave Creek. For the next few years Cave Creek was considered the new "secret" climbing spot. By 1992 the secret was out and the area quickly developed. *Stems and Seeds, Involuntary Manslaughter, The Big Easy* and *Skippy's Revenge* were some of the first routes to be done at Cave Creek.

HIDDEN WALLS

This bluff is not easily seen because of the trees that keep its view hidden from on top - but it is there. This bluff is located along the western border of Cave Creek and worth the very short approach.

1   **Whining Woody (10)** ★   Large offwidth at the end of bluff with a moderate top out. 35 feet. FFA: Frisbie 1992.

2   **Bitching and Moaning (7)** ★★   Left-angling crack, same top out as *Whining Woody*. 35 feet up, 30 feet sideways.

3   **Hairless Wonder (10 S)** ★   Follow crack up left on moderate climbing twenty feet. Start up a meandering thin crack that is tricky to protect. 55 feet. FFA: Frisbie/Delp/Hancock 1992.

4   **Resurrection (10)** ★★★★   Face climbing (5.9 PG) up dark colored rock leads to a short overhang halfway up the face.

Clay Frisbie on Involuntary Manslaughter (11–) ★★★★, Cave Creek. Photo: Ladd Campbell.

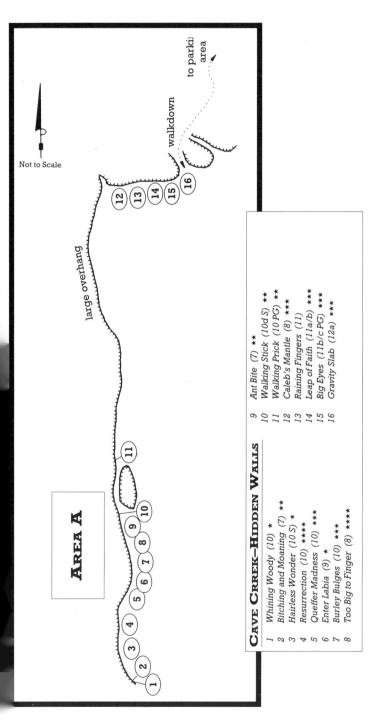

Not to Scale

to parki
area

walkdown

large overhang

AREA A

CAVE CREEK—HIDDEN WALLS

1 Whining Woody (10) ★
2 Bitching and Moaning (7) ★★
3 Hairless Wonder (10 S) ★
4 Resurrection (10) ★★★★
5 Queffer Madness (10) ★★★
6 Enter Labia (9) ★
7 Burley Bulges (10) ★★★
8 Too Big to Finger (8) ★★★★

9   Ant Bite (7) ★★
10 Walking Stick (10d S) ★★
11 Walking Prick (10 PG) ★★
12 Caleb's Mantle (8) ★★★
13 Raining Fingers (11)
14 Leap of Faith (11a/b) ★★★
15 Big Eyes (11b/c PG) ★★★
16 Gravity Slab (12a) ★★★

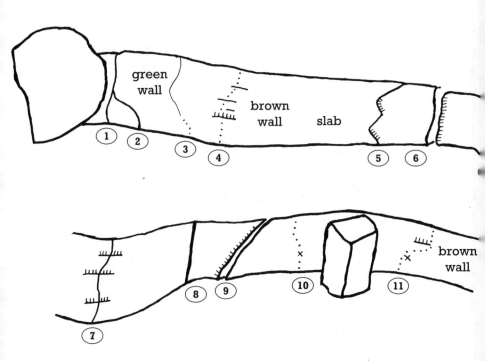

CAVE CRREK– HIDDEN WALLS

1	Whining Woody (10) ★
2	Bitching and Moaning (7) ★★
3	Hairless Wonder (10 S) ★
4	Resurrection (10) ★★★★
5	Queffer Madness (10) ★★★
6	Enter Labia (9) ★
7	Burley Bulges (10) ★★★

8	Too Big to Finger (8) ★★★★
9	Ant Bite (7) ★★
10	Walking Stick (10d S) ★★
11	Walking Prick (10 PG) ★★
12	Caleb's Mantle (8) ★★★
13	Raining Fingers (11)
14	Leap of Faith (11a/b) ★★★
15	Big Eyes (11b/c PG) ★★★
16	Gravity Slab (12a) ★★★

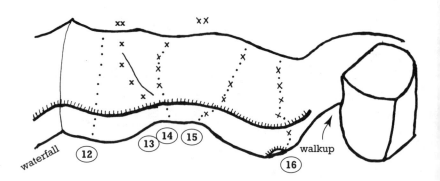

Above the overhang is an improbable looking thin seam. This route is truly a matchless traditional style face climb loaded with several 5.10 moves to contemplate and savor. It also accepts more protection than would be appear. 55 feet. FFA: Frisbie/Delp/Hancock 1992.

5   **Queffer Madness (10)** ★★★   Thin mossy overhanging handcrack; start out of cave with boulder move to obtain (5.10) good handcrack, above that leads to an overhanging fist crack and a ledge. Follow easy crack right. 55 feet. FFA: Woody Delp/Tom Hancock 1992.

6   **Enter Labia (9)** ★   Overhanging body size offwidth just right of *Queffer Madness.* 55 feet. FFA: Tom Hancock 1992.

7   **Burley Bulges (10)** ★★★   Winding crack with three short roofs, the last roof's the crux. 55 feet. FFA: Tom Hancock/Clay Frisbie 1992.

8   **Too Big to Finger (8)** ★★★★   This route is so obvious if you can't find it then you must be lost. Continuous right-facing fist-sized dihedral crack. Now all that is left to do is set your fists in motion. 45 feet. FFA: Mike Stites 1992.

9   **Ant Bite (7)** ★★   Classic handcrack that angles right. 45 feet. FFA: Frisbie 1992.

10   **Walking Stick (10d S)** ★★   Dark brown rock up to bolt then veer right above bolt. Small to mid-size tri-cam protects well above bolt. 45 feet. FFA: Clay Frisbie/Woody Delp 1992.

11   **Walking Prick (10 PG)** ★★   One bolt wonder face climb right of free standing boulder. 40 feet. FFA: Clay Frisbie/Woody Delp 1992.

12   **Caleb's Mantel (8)** ★★★   Twenty feet left of *Leap of Faith* where large holds allow passage through the roof system. For those vertically challenged this route provides the most moderate climbing in this area with several various crux moves to keep things interesting.

13   **Raining Fingers (11)**   Left diagonal crack that is terminally wet. Of course the degree of difficulty can vary depending on the degree of wetness. Four bolts, two-bolt anchor. FFA: ?, 1997.

14   **Leap of Faith (11a/b)** ★★★   Fifteen yards left of walkdown, climb overhanging face straight past four bolts and two-bolt rappel anchor. 55 feet. FFA: Clay Frisbie/Sean Burns 11/93.

15   **Big Eyes (11b/c PG)** ★★★   Climb up and right to first bolt. Continue up past three more bolts and a looped chickenhead. 55 feet. FFA: Hancock/Delp/Stites 1992.

16   **Gravity Slab (12a)** ★★★   Five yards left of walkdown, stick clip first bolt continue on past four more bolts on very overhanging rock, rappel anchor. 55 feet. FFA: Ken Cuddy/Burns/Frisbie 1993.

17   **Snake, Rattle and Roll (10d)** ★★★★   Fifty yards around corner right of walkdown. Climb red face on overhanging rock past five bolts and a fixed pin to a two-bolt anchor. Sustained climbing on large holds make for an enjoyable classic route. 65 feet. FFA: Gary Olsen 10/93.

18   **Thermonuclear Meltdown (11 S)** ★★   Thin crack in an orange, left-facing dihedral twenty feet right of *Snake, Rattle and Roll*. 60 feet. FFA: Mike Stites/Clay Frisbie 2/93.

19   **Wandering Spirit (9 PG)** ★★★★   Two-pitch route that begins at the corner left of *The Big Easy*. There are two ways to start: 1) start at the vertical orange face under the roof (5.10 PG); or 2) start on the left side taking the easiest path up loose rock to the base of the roof (5.7). Both lead to the large visor-shaped roof with a right- angling thin seam located under the roof. Second pitch (5.9) starts at the start of the thin seam and moves right under roof using small edges and side pulls. A pin is located twelve feet out from the belay. This can also be done in one pitch fairly easily if long slings are used. 50 feet up, 50 feet sideways and around. FFA: Mike Stites/Keith Smith 4/93.

20   **Flying Elvis (12a/b)** ★★★★   Just left of *The Big Easy*, climb a very constant overhang past six bolts to a two-bolt anchor. This route is so overhung it provides a great place to hide and climb during rain storms. 60 feet. FFA: Tony Mayse/Terry Andrews 4/94.

21   **The Big Easy (11 S–X)** ★★   Large dihedral nine-inch-wide crack ascends up at a 45° angle. This prominent looking route provides for a unique and distinctive offwidth with the crux move about 20 to 30 feet off the ground. Protection: Good protection at the bottom but the rest of the route is a long run out on 5.9 climbing, a Big Dude to slide up with you might possibly work. A couple of the bolts on *Flying Elvis* can be reached from *The Big Easy*, these bolts were not there originally. Using these bolts would manufacture considerably less of a pensive route. 65 feet. FFA: Clay Frisbie/Woody Delp 1990.

22   **Involuntary Manslaughter (11–)** ★★★★   Very prominent orange overhung wall with an unmistakable crack system that provides an exquisite sustained route just twenty feet right of *The Big Easy*. Start route by powering up fifteen feet on large edges to where the crack system begins. Use edges and crack for twenty more feet (5.11–) to reach large horizontal ledge. Continue route in a classic handcrack (5.10- sustained) to the top. Can be

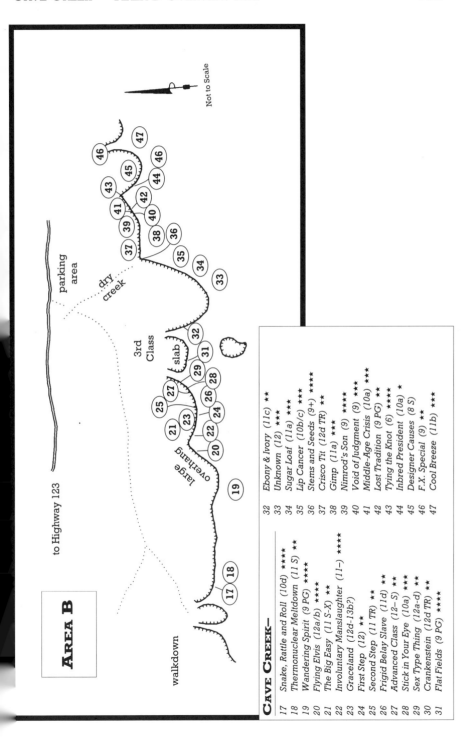

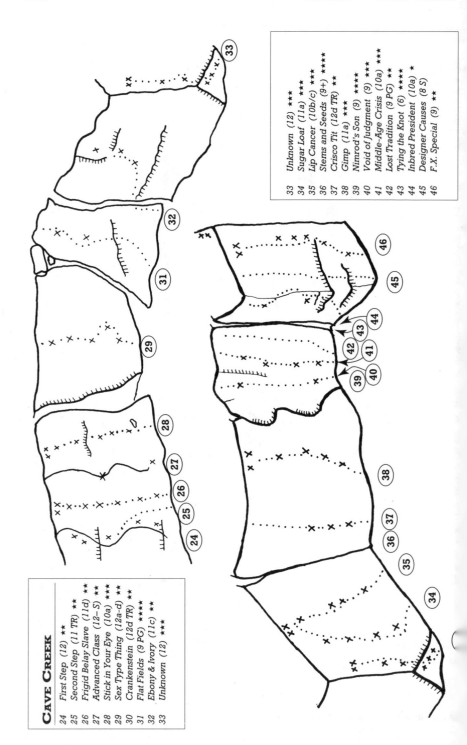

CAVE CREEK

24 First Step (12) **
25 Second Step (11 TR) **
26 Frigid Belay Slave (11d) **
27 Advanced Class (12–5) **
28 Stick in Your Eye (10a) ***
29 Sex Type Thing (12a-d) **
30 Crankenstein (12d TR) **
31 Flat Fields (9 PG) ****
32 Ebony & Ivory (11c) **
33 Unknown (12) ***

33 Unknown (12) ***
34 Sugar Loaf (11a) ***
35 Lip Cancer (10b/c) ***
36 Stems and Seeds (9+) ****
37 Crisco Tit (12d TR) **
38 Gimp (11a) ***
39 Nimrod's Son (9) ****
40 Void of Judgment (9) ***
41 Middle-Age Crisis (10a) ***
42 Lost Tradition (9 PG) **
43 Tying the Knot (6) ****
44 Inbred President (10a) *
45 Designer Causes (8 S)
46 F.X. Special (9) **

strenuous to protect the start, but for the rest of the route the protection is ample. This route is a traditional classic testpiece route for the Cave Creek area. 70 feet. FFA: Clay Frisbie/Woody Delp 1990.

23   **Graceland (12d-13b?)**   Very dynamic moves lead to first bolt, six bolts may need some gear? Crux move located at the bottom of route. 70 feet.

24   **First Step (12)** ★★   Boulder up overhang ten feet to a thin fingercrack. Turn the overhang (5.12) continue in the crack system with sustained moves for the entire climb. The inbetween finger-hand crack start of this route is more intricate and difficult than it may appear. Get ready for tight forearms and tweaked fingers. The first bolt is unfortunately a stick clip. Five bolts. 70 feet FFA: Clay Frisbie/Chuck Caughlin 3/94.

25   **Second Step (11 TR)** ★★   Start on the orange face between *First Step* and *Advanced Class* climbing up and left. This will intersect at the second roof (third bolt) on *First Step*. Finish on the last half of *First Step*. This is just an easier, less direct way to do *First Step* on top-rope.

26   **Frigid Belay Slave (11d)** ★★   Face between two crack systems, very sustained 5.10 climbing leads to a technical crux. Six bolts, two-bolt anchor. FFA: Tom Carter/Kim Milburn/Francis Connors 1996.

27   **Advanced Class (12– S)** ★★   Face climb on orange rock past a bolt to reach the thin serpentine crack that winds its way up the face. A fixed pin is located halfway up crack. The climbing is sustained and the pro is thin, bring a well-mixed rack. 70 feet. FFA: Frisbie/Delp/Hancock 1992.

28   **Stick in Your Eye (10a)** ★★★   Enjoyable face climb with five bolts. Starts at two obvious pockets. Two-bolt anchor. 45 feet. FFA: Gary Olsen 1993.

29   **Sex Type Thing (12a-d)** ★★   Very blank vertical face twenty yards left of third-class walkdown. Route starts directly in front of a tree almost touching the rock. Climb past five bolts to top. 50 feet. Climb is height dependent. FFA: Cuddy/Burns/Adam Dick 3/93.

30   **Crankenstein (12d TR)** ★★   The boulder down hill from *Flat Fields* has two anchors located on the top backside of the boulder. Top rope the steep backside of the boulder. At the start and crux of the route a spotter is essential because of the potential bad pendulum when top-roping.

31   **Flat Fields (9 PG)** ★★★★   Located on south-facing, low-angle slab, this route may look like an unabridged moderate line, but

several enjoyable 5.7 - 5.8 balance moves on thin protection lead to the first bolt. At the headwall the route continues with balance moves (5.9) past the second bolt to top out. Slab routes such as this are a unique find among all the vertical and overhanging lines that predominate the area, so savor the effortless energy of this route. This was the first route to see a bolt at Cave Creek. 55 feet. FFA: Woody Delp/Clay Frisbie 1991.

32   **Ebony & Ivory (11c)** ★★   Start in the wide crack on right side of the slab. Step right out of the crack on to the face to clip the first bolt. Three bolts and several technical moves make for enjoyable climbing up water-streaked wall. 45 feet. FFA: Clay Frisbie/Mike Stites 3/93.

33   **Unknown (12)** ★★★   Start on the overhanging arête, finish on the vertical face. Five bolts, two-bolt anchor. FFA: ? 1996.

34   **Sugar Loaf (11a)** ★★★   Climb straight up the black face on rounded edges. Four bolts, two-bolt anchor. 55 feet. FFA: Clay Frisbie/JR Chappell 12/96.

35   **Lip Cancer (10b/c)** ★★★   Fifteen feet left of *Stems and Seeds*. Boulder twenty feet to the first bolt and continue straight up and left with several pleasant moves on sloping holds. Protection from one to two inches can be found between the third and fourth bolts. Two-bolt anchor. 55 feet. FFA: Mike Stites/Clay Frisbie 3/93.

36   **Stems and Seeds (9+)** ★★★★   Unmistakable classic thin dihedral crack where two black walls come together. Climb dihedral via stem and mantels (5.9+). Although this route is short it is quite enjoyable all the way up with interesting stemming moves. [When Woody Delp first brought me to his (new, very secret) area he purposely walked past this outstanding dihedral as if he knew it didn't exist. I threw down my pack and demanded "Are you blind? We have to climb this route." Woody let go a large laugh because that is exactly what he had planned all along. The rest is history. This is the first route that I had the pleasure of climbing at Cave Creek.] This route is prone to wetness during the spring. 55 feet. FFA: Woody Delp/Clay Frisbie 1990.

37   **Crisco Tit (12d TR)** ★★   Ten feet right of *Stems and Seeds*. Climb very blank grey face with extremely thin sequential moves. This route appears to still be a project.

38   **Gimp (11a)** ★★★   Thin crack/face on black rock: four bolts make for a well-protected strenuous climb. This route originally started out as a boulder problem. Two-bolt anchor. 35 feet. FFA: Frisbie/Stites/Hancock 3/93.

39   **Nimrod's Son (9) ★★★★**   Enjoyable overhanging handcrack (5.8) at the bottom of the route leads to a left-facing thin dihedral crack (5.9) to top out. 45 feet. FFA: Woody Delp 1990.

40   **Void of Judgment (9) ★★★**   Face right of *Nimrod's Son* climb up middle of wall on pencil size edges that become jugs at the concave face area on top. This route is a 5.9 route with a 5.10 boulder start. Two bolts. 45 feet. FFA: Robin Coleman 1991 Clay Frisbie 1990.

41   **Middle-Age Crisis (10a) ★★★**   Four bolts up smooth face between *Void of Judgment* and *Tying the Knot.* 45 feet. FFA: Tom Carter/Kim Milburn/Francis Connors 1996.

42   **Lost Tradition (9 PG) ★★**   Light green face between *Middle-Age Crisis* and *Tying The Knot* taking the path of least resistance. Protection is bleak for the start. 45 feet. FFA: Dennis Nelms 1991.

43   **Tying the Knot (6) ★★★★**   Left-facing large dihedral crack that is full of enjoyable climbing, good place to use that oversized gear that is gathering dust. 55 feet. FFA: Barry Gilbert/Scott Brandt 1992.

44   **Inbred President (10a) ★**   Arête with two bolts. Same start as *Tying the Knot,* then traverse right under overhang. A one- to two-inch crack pocket provides bomber protection for the crux to turn the overhang on the arête. 55 feet. FFA: Sean Burns/Justin Mullins 1994.

45   **Designer Causes (8 S)**   Just right of arête, ascend up middle of face on jug holds. Beware of rotten orange rock at the start. 55 feet. FFA: Clay Frisbie/Neil Sade 1995.

46   **F.X. Special (9) ★★**   Five bolts up orange face, two-bolt anchor. 55 feet. FFA: Tom Carter/Kim Milburn/Francis Connors 1996.

47   **Cool Breeze (11b) ★★★**   If you feel the cool breeze coming out of the offwidth chimney, you are at the right spot. Climb a steep face left of chimney just above small cave. After fourth bolt, move left past fixed pin then up jugs to a two-bolt anchor left around the corner. 60 feet. FFA: Sean Burns 2/94.

48   **Breeze Way (9) ★**   Chimney and offwidth that intersects with *Cool Breeze* after the lip of the overhang then continue straight up. 55 feet. FFA: Clay Frisbie/Chuck Caughlin 3/94.

49   **Chos Man (10a) ★★★**   Twenty feet right of *Breeze Way.* Orange face with eight bolts, two-bolt anchor. 70 feet. FFA: Frisbie/Hancock/Caughlin 1996.

50   **Buddhist Prodigy (11a) ★★**   Overhanging orange rock leads to white colored rock with four bolts and two-bolt anchor. 45 feet. FFA: Sean Burns.

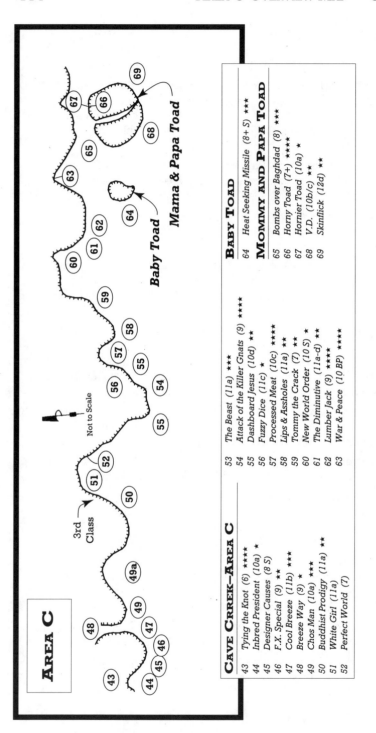

AREA C

3rd Class

Not to Scale

Baby Toad

Mama & Papa Toad

CAVE CREEK–AREA C

43 Tying the Knot (6) ★★★★
44 Inbred President (10a) ★
45 Designer Causes (8 S)
46 F.X. Special (9) ★★
47 Cool Breeze (11b) ★★★
48 Breeze Way (9) ★
49 Chos Man (10a) ★★★
50 Buddhist Prodigy (11a) ★★
51 White Girl (11a)
52 Perfect World (7)

53 The Beast (11a) ★★★
54 Attack of the Killer Gnats (9) ★★★★
55 Dashboard Jesus (10d) ★★
56 Fuzzy Dice (11c) ★
57 Processed Meat (10c) ★★★★
58 Lips & Assholes (11a)
59 Tommy the Crack (7) ★★
60 New World Order (10 S) ★
61 The Diminutive (11a-d) ★★
62 Lumber Jack (9) ★★★★
63 War & Peace (10 BP) ★★★★

BABY TOAD

64 Heat Seeking Missile (8+ S) ★★★

MOMMY AND PAPA TOAD

65 Bombs over Baghdad (8) ★★★
66 Horny Toad (7+) ★★★★
67 Hornier Toad (10a) ★
68 V.D. (10b/c) ★★
69 Skinflick (12d) ★★

51 White Girl (11a)   White, short, face climb with three bolts. Take the path of least resistance without going too far to the right. Two-bolt anchor. 35 feet. FFA: Sean Burns/Howie Benyon 3/94.

52 Perfect World (7)   Short dihedral handcrack. 20 feet.

53 The Beast (11a) ★★★   Brown, pocketed, bulgy face. Brown hangers, four bolts and a two-bolt anchor. Don't miss the second clip. 60 feet. FFA: Olsen/Burns/Alex Weston 11/93.

54 Attack of the Killer Gnats (9) ★★★★   Boulder up fifteen feet to the base of an obvious slightly overhanging handcrack that provides strenuous climbing and a splendid opportunity to use those active cam devices. Let the jamming begin! On that hot, muggy, summer day one might venture to guess what happened during the first ascent. Gnats, chiggers, horseflies, blood-sucking ticks and whatever else. They all have their good days and bad days too. 55 feet. FFA: Woody Delp/Tom Hancock 1992.

55 Dashboard Jesus (10d) ★★   Boulder up to steep grey face three bolts to a two-bolt anchor. One-inch pro protects the start. This route is harder than it looks with some devious holds. 45 feet. FFA: Cuddy/Burns/Dick 3/93.

56 Fuzzy Dice (11c) ★   Same start as *Dashboard Jesus* then move right. This route has a technical sequence crux on obscure devious holds. Four bolts, Two-bolt anchor. FFA: Tom Carter/Kim Milburn/Francis Connors 1996.

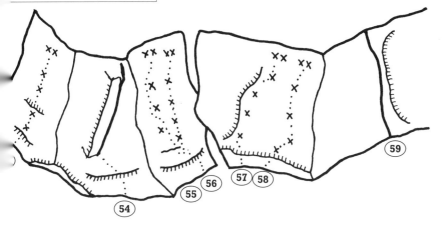

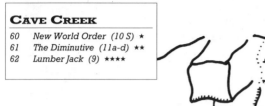

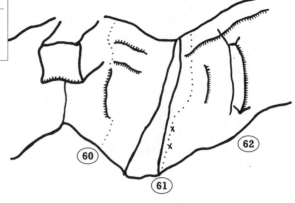

CAVE CREEK

60   *New World Order (10 S)* ★
61   *The Diminutive (11a-d)* ★★
62   *Lumber Jack (9)* ★★★★

57   **Processed Meat (10c)** ★★★★   Overhanging flake system on orange rock. Interesting climbing past four bolts to a two-bolt anchor. 50 feet. FFA: Burns/Dick/Cuddy 3/93.

58   **Lips & Assholes (11a)** ★★   Climb an orange overhanging face with dynamic moves on large holds past five bolts to a two-bolt anchor. FFA: Stites/Cuddy/Burns/Dick 4/94.

59   **Tommy the Crack (7)** ★★   Straight-in crack right around corner from *Processed Meat*. 30 feet. FFA: Dick/Alexander.

60   **New World Order (10 S)** ★   Middle of face, ten feet left of arête. Face climb straight up and left. Protection is poor after the crux. 50 feet. FFA: Clay Frisbie/Woody Delp 1991.

61   **The Diminutive (11a-d)** ★★   Starts on the arête just left of *Lumber Jack*. A few technical moves lead past two bolts. Continue with moderate face climbing to the top. Climb is height dependent. 55 feet. FFA: Chad Davis/Clay Frisbie 1996.

62   **Lumber Jack (9)** ★★★★   Conspicuous fingercrack next to cedar tree devises a superior route. 55 feet. FFA: Woody Delp/Clay Frisbie 1990.

63   **War & Peace (10 BP)** ★★★★   Location is the wall north of Baby Toad Boulder. Twenty-foot dihedral fingercrack leads to a large roof system above. The first twenty feet of this dihedral is a classic boulder problem. To retreat, downclimb the same moves.

BABY TOAD

64   **Heat Seeking Missile (8+ S)** ★★★   Triangular face on the west side of the boulder. Climb up middle of slightly orange face with good flakes for holds. 40 feet. FFA: Clay Frisbie 2/91

The masterful Woody Delp on War & Peace (5.10 BP) ★★★★,
Cave Creek. Photo: Woody Delp Collection.

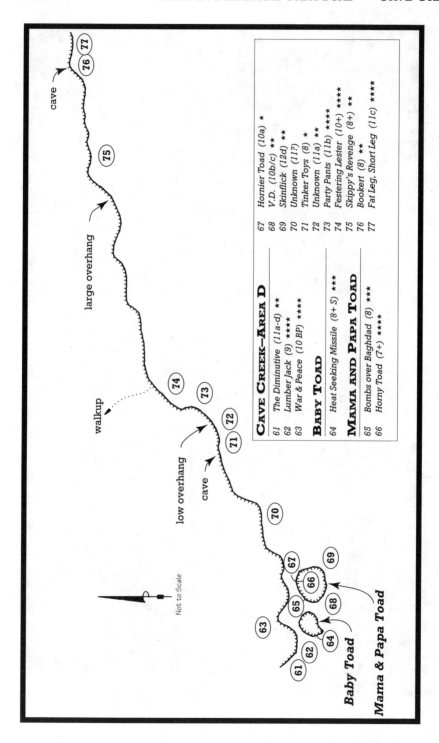

CAVE CREEK–AREA D

61   The Diminutive (11a–d) ★★
62   Lumber Jack (9) ★★★★
63   War & Peace (10 BP) ★★★★

BABY TOAD

64   Heat Seeking Missile (8+ S) ★★★

MAMA AND PAPA TOAD

65   Bombs over Baghdad (8) ★★★
66   Horny Toad (7+) ★★★★

67   Hornier Toad (10a) ★
68   V.D. (10b/c) ★★
69   Skinflick (12d) ★★
70   Unknown (11?)
71   Tinker Toys (8) ★
72   Unknown (11a) ★★
73   Party Pants (11b) ★★★★
74   Festering Lester (10+) ★★★★
75   Skippy's Revenge (8+) ★★
76   Bookert (8) ★★
77   Fat Leg, Short Leg (11c) ★★★★

cave

large overhang

walkup

low overhang

cave

Not to Scale

Baby Toad

Mama & Papa Toad

MAMA AND PAPA TOAD

65   **Bombs over Baghdad (8)** ★★★   On north side of Mommy Toad, start with right-angling crack that juts back left then continue up the moderate face to top. 40 feet. FFA: Clay Frisbie 2/91.

66   **Horny Toad (7+)** ★★★★   Crack in the middle of the north-facing side of boulder. Traverse right under headwall to climb off the boulder. 40 feet. FFA: Clay Frisbie 2/91.

67   **Hornier Toad (10a)** ★   Same as Horny Toad. At the headwall, instead of traversing right, climb straight up past a bolt on the head wall to top out on the boulder. 55 feet. FFA: Clay Frisbie/Mike Stites 3/93.

68   **V.D. (10b/c)** ★★   Located on back side of boulder. Climb past five bolts on positive holds to an open cold-shut anchor in the middle of the face. 35 feet, 55 feet. FFA: Virgil Davis 1994.

69   **Skinflick (12d)** ★★   Located on back side of boulder, protruding overhang. Their are two versions of this route: 1) struggle up to overhang with three bolts; 2) second version of this route shares the first two bolts then traverses right with an undercling and another bolt. 40 feet. FFA: Terry Andrews 1995.

70   **Unknown (11?)**   Orange face with one bolt low, leads to thin cracks above? Could be unfinished route or just very unpleasant.

71   **Tinker Toys (8)** ★   Start on arête where it is accessible to get on the face before it drops off with an overhang. A lot of 5.6 climbing leads to one crux move at the roof near the top. 75 feet. FFA: Clay Frisbie/Neil Sade 8/95.

72   **Unknown (11a)** ★★   Face just left of massive overhang. Jug haul up short steep white and green face past three bolts. Two-bolt anchor. 40 feet. FFA: ? 1996.

73   **Party Pants (11b)** ★★★★   Black face with seven bolts and a two-bolt anchor on top. Several crux moves and sustained climbing make the climbing very captivating. The only thing that could make this route better is more of it. 75 feet. FFA: Tony Morris 8/95.

74   **Festering Lester (10+)** ★★★★   Twenty-foot, fist-and-hand-size roof crack on the left side of the walkdown. Start from ledge directly into the roof. This obscure little sleeper of a climb does not look like much but it is a full on, power packed, fist-and-hand jam roof crack. Twenty feet of climbing on this unique roof crack will feel more like a full rope length of climbing as you burp, fart and scratch your way around this massive roof. This is classic Arkansas roof climbing at its foremost with time-honored hand jams and enough uncomfortable, peculiar positions to provide a memorable experience for all. This route is prone to be wet. Best to catch it during a dry spell. FFA: Tom Hancock/Woody Delp 1993.

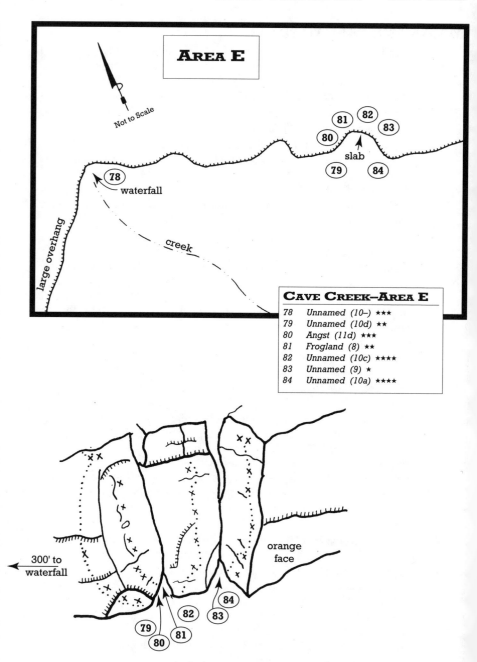

AREA E

Not to Scale

waterfall

slab

large overhang

creek

CAVE CREEK–AREA E

78 Unnamed (10–) ★★★
79 Unnamed (10d) ★★
80 Angst (11d) ★★★
81 Frogland (8) ★★
82 Unnamed (10c) ★★★★
83 Unnamed (9) ★
84 Unnamed (10a) ★★★★

300' to
waterfall

orange
face

75   **Skippy's Revenge (8+)** ★★   Two 5.8+ moves lead thin to a
      crack (5.8). At large ledge jog left to easier climbing or continue
      straight up and turn bulge (5.10). FFA: Mike Giner/Woody Delp
      1990.

76   **Bookert (8)** ★★. Dihedral crack located above cave. Same start
      as *Fat Leg, Short Leg*. Continue in dihedral with an enjoyable
      handcrack that leads to the top.

77   **Fat Leg, Short Leg (11c)** ★★★★   Orange face with a cave
      located at the base. Start route on the left side of cave, traverse
      right along ledge to gain access to the orange face. At the second
      bolt there are two ways to do the route from here: 1) Traverse
      right to climb into the triangular dihedral (5.11c) to gain access to
      the large horizontal crack; 2) Climb straight above the second
      bolt over the small overhang with very dynamic moves (5.12a) to
      gain access to the large horizontal crack. From the horizontal
      crack enjoy a no-hands rest before being thrust into the heart of
      the route. A pumpfest (5.11b) with some interesting climbing will
      carry you to the top. Extra long runners on the bottom few bolts
      will help minimize rope drag. Two bolt anchor. 80 feet. FFA: Tony
      Morris 1995.

78   **Unnamed (10–)** ★★★   Crack system right of waterfall. Can be
      done in two pitches.90 feet. FFA: Tony Morris/Kerry Allen 1995.

79   **Unnamed (10d)** ★★   Overhanging arête on the left wall. A
      jugfest with dynamic moves leads through the overhang with
      moderate climbing to the top. Five bolts. 70 feet. FFA: Tony
      Morris.

80   **Angst (11d)** ★★★   Intermittent crack system located in the
      middle of the left vertical wall. Several technical moves with
      sustained climbing make for a striking lead up this taxing route.
      Six bolts. 60 feet. FFA: Clay Frisbie/J.R. Chappel 1996.

81   **Frogland (8)** ★★   Left corner crack system. 70 feet. FFA: Ladd
      Campbell

82   **Unnamed (10c)** ★★★★   Sixty-foot slab located between two
      walls. Superb face climbing up slab with several intriguing
      technical moves (5.10c) leads to a roof crack at the top for a
      stimulating finish. An Arkansas classic. 70 feet. FFA: Tony Morris
      1995.

83   **Unnamed (9)** ★   Right corner crack system. 70 feet.

84   **Unnamed (10a)** ★★★★   Arête located on the right wall. Stem up
      between two walls to attain the first bolt. Stimulating climbing with
      several moves leads up the arête past four more bolts and a two-
      bolt anchor. 60 feet. FFA: Tony Morris 1995.

*A climber on the ultra classic Poison Ivy (5.7+) ★★★★
Poison Ivy Wall (p.82) Photo: Woody Delp Collection.*

CHAPTER FIVE

RICKETT'S MOUNTAIN AREA

This area has a vast amount of rock but has seen very little climbing. Along Farm Road 1204, it is located six miles from Highway 7 at Cowell or 10.3 grueling miles uphill from Mt. Judea. Rickett's Mountain currently includes the Land of the Little People, Fraggle Rock and Fern Gully. Land of the Little People can easily be seen from the road in the winter after all the leaves are off the trees.

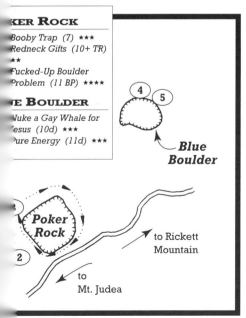

KER ROCK

Booby Trap (7) ★★★
Redneck Gifts (10+ TR)
★★
Fucked-Up Boulder
Problem (11 BP) ★★★★

E BOULDER

Nuke a Gay Whale for
Jesus (10d) ★★★
Pure Energy (11d) ★★★

Blue Boulder

Poker Rock

to Rickett Mountain

to Mt. Judea

POKER ROCK

Poker Rock is the boulder that is located halfway between Mt. Judea and Rickett's Mountain along Farm Road 1204. This boulder protrudes out into the road and has had the bumper of more than one car plow into it. With four sides, this boulder has superb bouldering on a couple of the faces. Poker Rock received its name from the locals. It was a known amusement spot for playing poker and gambling. From atop the boulder, they could easily spot anyone coming and make a quick getaway.

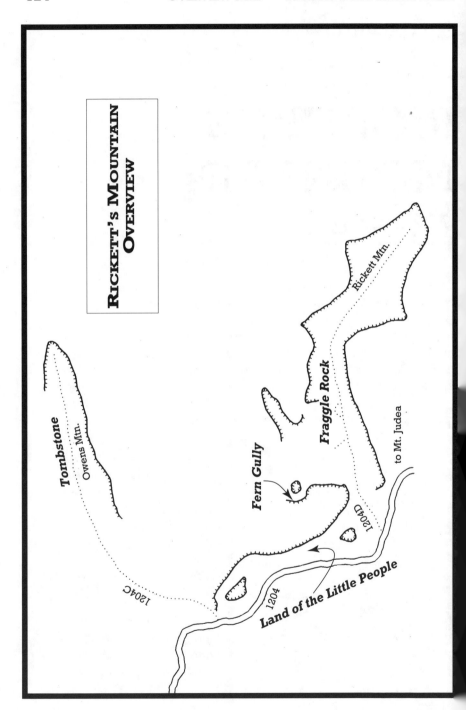

1   **Booby Trap (7)** ★★★   South side of boulder just left of the arête follow the line of jugs and positive edges. 40 feet.

2   **Redneck Gifts (10+ TR)** ★★   Middle of wall on east side of boulder one bolt and anchor at top. 30 feet.

3   **Fucked-Up Boulder Problem (11 BP)** ★★★★   Traverse the whole boulder starting where the boulder protrudes into the road (northeast corner) traverse right around the boulder leaving the pumpy north face for the finish (crux).

BLUE BOULDER

Blue Boulder is located one hundred yards up the hill from Poker Rock. There is an old blue car on the south side of the road that marks the spot (if the car is still there). Blue Boulder is on the south side of the road about one hundred feet out in the woods.

4   **Nuke a Gay Whale for Jesus (10d)** ★★★   South side of the boulder up arête with three bolts and a two-bolt anchor. 40 feet. FFA: Clay Frisbie/Tom Hancock 8/95.

5   **Pure Energy (11d)** ★★★   South side of the boulder. Start on the left side of the smooth arête moving up and left. Several powerful intricate moves on less than positive holds make this a captivating route. Five bolts, two-bolt anchor. 45 feet. FFA: Clay Frisbie/Chuck Caughlin 1995.

FRAGGLE ROCK

Located high atop Rickett's Mountain a quarter-mile off Farm Road 1204 is Fraggle Rock. This is one of the finest bouldering spots in northern Arkansas with many boulders scattered throughout the area. A very small but superb camping area is situated among the boulders. Like other areas, the climbing is good year round. Unlike other areas, the rock dries almost immediately after a good rain due to the fact that these are boulders not bluffs. Some of the routes in this area are recommend as lead or top rope but the vast majority of climbing is on twenty-foot boulders with good landings. I have listed some problems but basically the bouldering is as good as one's imagination. One only need to look to find or devise a good or enjoyable boulder problem. This area is also popular with the locals so don't be surprised to see four-wheelers buzzing about.

1   **Stuck in High Gear (9 BP)** ★★★★   Cave along the road fifty yards up from the main camping. Start in back of cave with roof crack. Step off rock platform for the first airy crux continue out crack to lip. Turn lip via weird (5.9) offwidth moves for top out.

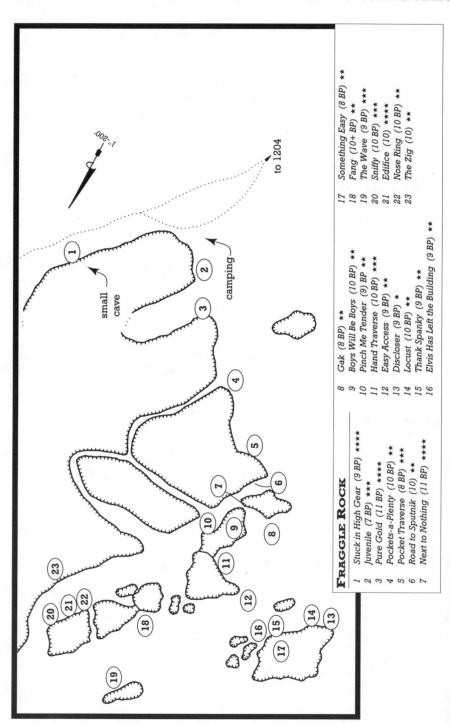

FRAGGLE ROCK

1   Stuck in High Gear (9 BP) ★★★★
2   Juvenile (7 BP) ★★★
3   Pure Gold (11 BP) ★★★★
4   Pockets-a-Plenty (10 BP) ★★
5   Pocket Traverse (8 BP) ★★★
6   Road to Sputnik (10) ★★
7   Next to Nothing (11 BP) ★★★★

8   Gak (8 BP) ★★
9   Boys Will Be Boys (10 BP) ★★
10   Pinch Me Tender (9) BP ★★
11   Hand Traverse (10 BP) ★★★
12   Easy Access (9 BP) ★★
13   Discloser (9 BP) ★
14   Locust (10 BP) ★★
15   Thank Spanky (9 BP) ★★
16   Elvis Has Left the Building (9 BP) ★★

17   Something Easy (8 BP) ★★
18   Fang (10+ BP) ★★
19   The Wave (9 BP) ★★★
20   Sniffy (10 BP) ★★★
21   Edifice (10) ★★★★
22   Nose Ring (10 BP) ★★
23   The Zig (10) ★★

small cave

camping

to 1204

1"=200'

2   **Juvenile (7 BP)** ★★★   Boulder straight up on jugs

3   **Pure Gold (11 BP)** ★★★★   Traverse low to the ground from right to left in horizontal crack under overhang on orange rock. The trick is not letting your feet touch the ground. "The Munchkin Traverse" might be a more appropriate title. This is also a great place to bivy!

4   **Pockets-a-Plenty (10 BP)** ★★   Straight up middle of overhanging face.

5   **Pocket Traverse (8 BP)** ★★★   Traverse from left to right.

6   **Road to Sputnik (10)** ★★   Fingercrack at top. Due to a bad landing a rope might come in handy. FFA: Stacy Fairbanks.

7   **Next to Nothing (11 BP)** ★★★★   Overhanging arête.

8   **Gak (8 BP)** ★★   Pocket face down right from *Next to Nothing*.

9   **Boys Will Be Boys (10 BP)** ★★   Short arête.

10   **Pinch Me Tender (9) BP** ★★   Face.

11   **Hand Traverse (10 BP)** ★★★   Traverse either way in crack under roof.

12   **Easy Access (9 BP)** ★★   Short arête to the top.

13   **Discloser (9 BP)** ★   Left end of boulder, climb straight up.

14   **Locust (10 BP)** ★★   Climb straight up face.

15   **Thank Spanky (9 BP)** ★★   Use crack at the top.

16   **Elvis Has Left the Building (9 BP)** ★★   Same route as *Thank Spanky* except do not use crack at the top.

17   **Something Easy (8 BP)** ★★   Traverse face.

18   **Fang (10+ BP)** ★★   Climb high on arête then traverse down right to the end.

19   **The Wave (9 BP)** ★★★   Horizontal crack traverse.

20   **Sniffy (10 BP)** ★★★   Hand traverse out to lip, then pull lip to the top of boulder.

21   **Edifice (10)** ★★★★   Twenty-five-foot, slightly overhung handcrack that narrows to a fingercrack at the top. Great short lead with the crux at the top. FFA: Clay Frisbie\Tom Hancock.

22   **Nose Ring (10 BP)** ★★   Start in middle of face with crux moves at bottom and top. Long reaches on rounded jug holds (sustained 5.9) climbing leads to the top of the boulder. This is a very committing boulder problem.

23   **The Zig (10)** ★★   An intermittent crack that is hands-to-fingers-to-flaring-fist near the top. FFA: Tom Hancock/Eric Inman.

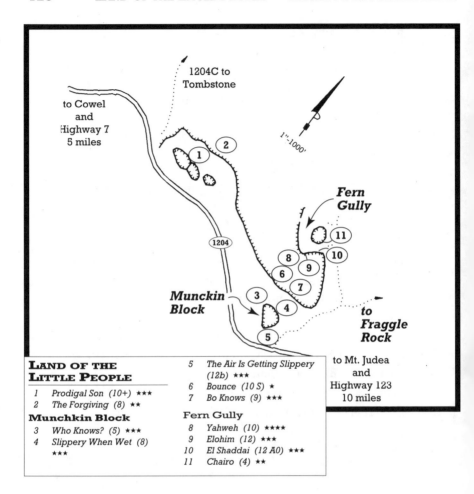

LAND OF THE LITTLE PEOPLE

1	Prodigal Son (10+) ★★★
2	The Forgiving (8) ★★

Munchkin Block

3	Who Knows? (5) ★★★
4	Slippery When Wet (8) ★★★

5	The Air Is Getting Slippery (12b) ★★★
6	Bounce (10 S) ★
7	Bo Knows (9) ★★★

Fern Gully

8	Yahweh (10) ★★★★
9	Elohim (12) ★★★
10	El Shaddai (12 A0) ★★★
11	Chairo (4) ★★

LAND OF THE LITTLE PEOPLE

Located atop Rickett's Mountain at Farm Road 1204 and 1204D. Most of the routes in this area receive very little sun. This area is easily approached in five minutes from 1204. The most prominent feature here is Munchkin Block, a large free-standing boulder, about one hundred feet from the road.

1   **Prodigal Son (10+)** ★★★   Chimney roof crack. FFA: Chuck Caughlin/Tom Hancock.

2   **The Forgiving (8)** ★★   Dihedral handcrack. FFA: Chuck Caughlin/Tom Hancock

MUNCHKIN BLOCK

3   **Who Knows?** (5) ★★★   Easiest section of climbing on the block up an intermittent crack system on the west face. FFA: Chuck Caughlin/Lou Stevenson 1993.

4   **Slippery When Wet** (8) ★★★   Crack in the middle of the face on the north side of the block. FFA: Chuck Caughlin/Lou Stevenson 1993.

5   **The Air Is Getting Slippery** (12b) ★★★   On the east side of the block is a predominant overhang that can be seen from the road when the leaves are down. This route weaves its way through the large roof system. Start with thin balancey face moves up white rock that leads to the large roof. At the roof traverse left to overcome and mount the overhang (5.12). After the traverse be prepared to make quick powerful moves. Nine bolts and a two-bolt anchor protect this interesting and difficult line. 65 feet. FFA: Frisbie/Hancock/Caughlin.

6   **Bounce** (10 S) ★   Face with boulder problem start leads to crack above. FFA: Clay Frisbie.

7   **Bo Knows** (9) ★★★   Located directly north of Munchkin Block is a twenty-foot roof crack that widens to an offwidth at the top. This route does contain some possible loose rock but is well worth the effort with a good assortment of interesting climbing. FFA: Chuck Caughlin/Lou Stevenson 1993.

FERN GULLY

Fern Gully, named for the ferns that grow there, receives no sun and is susceptible to wetness. The best time to climb here is summer and fall, anytime when the ground is dry and the air is warm. On Farm Road 1204D before reaching Fraggle Rock go a short way and turn left at closed lumber road and park where the road is blocked off. Hike along lumber road for 300 yards, look for bluff and free-standing block on the left about 100 yards up the hill through the trees. This is a very small area with a few hard routes. The route Yahweh by itself is well worth the fifteen-minute approach to Fern Gully. This is a "must do" if you are in the Rickett's Mountain area.

8   **Yahweh** (10) ★★★★   The predominant dihedral, fist-and-hand crack. A #4 Camalot works wonders at the five-inch crack crux section. Watch for possible loose rock near the top of the route. 80 feet. FFA: Clay Frisbie/Tom Hancock.

9   **Elohim** (12) ★★★   Boulder up fifteen feet to a left-angling fingercrack(5.11). From fingercrack, move up and left past several horizontal cracks till first bolt(5.11). Climb past four bolts (5.12), through a large almost detached flake. The fifth and final

bolt near the top protects the exit moves (5.11– but will probably feel more like 5.12 at this point) to the two-bolt belay anchor. This power draining route is a very demanding lead because of the sustained nature of the climbing. This route is known for causing a peculiar virus with symptoms of general fatigue, aching muscles (especially in the forearm region) and a loss of interest in climbing. If you exhibit these symptoms, don't worry, it is only a twenty-four-hour virus. The best remedy is plenty of rest. The best known antidote is to have a large ape factor and climb quickly. 70 feet. FFA: Frisbie/Hancock/Sheier.

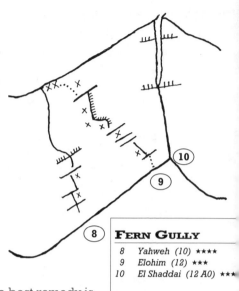

FERN GULLY

8	Yahweh (10) ****
9	Elohim (12) ***
10	El Shaddai (12 A0) ***

10   **El Shaddai (12 A0) ★★★**   The most obvious feature of this route is the fifty-foot fistcrack at the top of the route. Thin fingercrack at the bottom leads (5.10) up twenty feet to a bolt. Aid through this section by using the bolt. The aid stops at the point of standing on the first bolt. The first bolt is the only spot of aid on the route. Some desperate under clings and small holds (5.12) lead through the small jutting arête and the second bolt to join the fistcrack above. Forty feet of some interesting fist-and-hand jams (5.11–) entice to the two-bolt anchor above. Undoubtedly the spot of aid used on this route will go free at a higher degree of difficulty. The purpose of using aid on this route was not necessarily to develop an extremely difficult route, but instead to attain the enticing fistcrack above using as much free climbing as possible. 70 feet. FFA: Frisbie/Hancock/Caughlin.

11   **Chairo (4) ★★**   Easiest path up backside of block. 70 feet.

TOMBSTONE

Located at the end of Farm Road 1204C. Many ruts and ditches along these two miles make this area best approached with a four-wheel-drive. This peninsula on Owens Mountain is a large expanse of rock that hosts only a handful of established routes but bears ample potential. The camping here is enjoyable with superb scenic views but limited in space. A rappel at the end

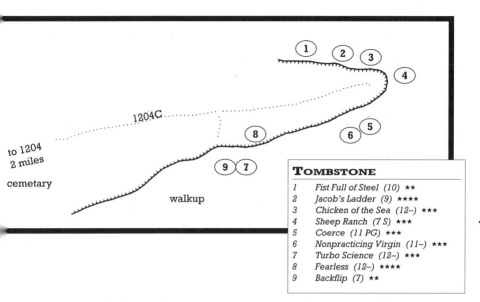

TOMBSTONE

1   Fist Full of Steel (10) ★★
2   Jacob's Ladder (9) ★★★★
3   Chicken of the Sea (12–) ★★★
4   Sheep Ranch (7 S) ★★★
5   Coerce (11 PG) ★★★
6   Nonpracticing Virgin (11–) ★★★
7   Turbo Science (12–) ★★★
8   Fearless (12–) ★★★★
9   Backflip (7) ★★

of the peninsula is the simplest approach to most of the routes. Walkouts can be easily found from the base of the cliff but not so easily found from on top.

1   **Fist Full of Steel (10)** ★★   Obvious fistcrack. 50 feet. FFA: Chuck Coughlin/Tom Hancock 10/93.

2   **Jacob's Ladder (9)** ★★★★   Prominent fingercrack with face holds mark this distinct and classic line. Start by bouldering up to gain access to the face. 60 feet. FFA: Unknown.

3   **Chicken of the Sea (12–)** ★★★   An immense roof crack with a fixed stopper make for a bizarre and difficult route. FFA: Frisbie/Hancock 1993.

4   **Sheep Ranch (7 S)** ★★★   Path of least resistance up face.

5   **Coerce (11 PG)** ★★★   Offwidth-chimney with one bolt. FFA: Clay Frisbie/Chuck Caughlin 11/93.

6   **Nonpracticing Virgin (11–)** ★★★   Arête with three bolts. FFA: Clay Frisbie/Chuck Caughlin 11/93.

7   **Turbo Science (12–)** ★★★   Arête two bolts (5.10) leads to *Fearless*. FFA: Clay Frisbie/Chuck Caughlin 11/93.

8   **Fearless (12–)** ★★★★   Left-facing dihedral then left under a roof leads to Yosemite-style fingercrack. Only thing that would make this route better is one hundred more feet. FFA: Frisbie/Delp/Hancock/Caughlin 11/93.

9   **Backflip (7)** ★★   Dihedral crack tops out under large roof. FFA: Tod Johnson 1993.

*Keith Smith on Hamburger Helper
(5.9) ★★★★, Blind Man's Bluff.
Photo: Billy Bisswanger Collection.*

GLOSSARY

Below are some of the terms used in this guide.

arête   An outside corner that produces a spine or ridge.

BA   Baby angle; a type of piton.

bouldery   Indicates crux moves located at the start of a route.

bomber   Absolute secure protection or big hand hold.

bomb bay chimney   A chimney crack that is so overhung or horizontal one must traverse for a distance inside the chimney.

dihedral   An inside corner.

crimper   A very small positive hold.

crux   The hardest section or move of a climb.

chimney   A crack large enough for a body to fit into.

chickenhead   A large protruding hold shaped like a doorknob.

fingercrack   A ¾" crack suitable to fit fingers in.

fistcrack   A three- to four-inch crack suitable to fit a fist in.

handcrack or jamcrack   Usually refers to a one-and-a-half to two-and-a-half-inch crack suitable to fit a hand into.

KB   Knifeblade; a type of thin piton.

LA   Lost arrow; a type of piton.

lieback   A climbing technique of pulling with the hands while pushing with feet.

offwidth   A crack too large for a fistjam (over three inches and under one foot) and too narrow to fit body into. A wide crack.

protection   Equipment placed in cracks or features of rock for anchors and safety during lead climbing.

slab   Low-angling rock face.

sloper   Rounded hold that does not have a positive edge.

stem   To bridge between two surfaces; common technique used in a dihedral.

stick clip   A method of clipping the first piece of protection on a route before leaving the ground. Usually a runner is taped to a stick to reach up and clip the piece. This is consider bad style unless it was the way the route was established; and then sometimes it is still considered bad style.

thin   A climb of relatively featureless holds usually requiring quick movement over small holds. When referring to a crack it is a usually smaller than a fingertip.

traverse   To move or climb sideways, without altitude gain.

*Clay Frisbee on Painted Warrior
(5.12-) ★★★★, The Painted Wall.
Photo: Billy Bisswanger Collection.*

INDEX

Bolded numbers refer to either topos, maps or photos of the route; rock features are listed in all capitals.

ACCESS: It's every climber's concer

The Access Fund, a national, non-profit climbers organization, works to k climbing areas open and to conserve the climbing environment. Need help closures? land acquisition? legal or land management issues? funding for trails other projects? starting a local climbers' group? CALL US!

Climbers can help preserve access by being committed to Leave No Tr (minimum-impact) practices. Here are some simple guidelines:

• **ASPIRE TO "LEAVE NO TRACE"** especially in environmentally sensitive areas caves. Chalk can be a significant impact on dark and porous rock – don't use it aro historic rock art. Pick up litter, and leave trees and plants intact.

• **DISPOSE OF HUMAN WASTE PROPERLY** Use toilets whenever possible. If to are not available, dig a "cat hole" at least six inches deep and 200 feet from any wa trails, campsites, or the base of climbs. *Always pack out toilet paper.* On big wall rou use a "poop tube" and carry waste up and off with you (the old "bag toss" is now illega many areas).

• **USE EXISTING TRAILS** Cutting switchbacks causes erosion. When walking off-tr tread lightly, especially in the desert where cryptogamic soils (usually a dark crust) t thousands of years to form and are easily damaged. Be aware that "rim ecologies" clifftop) are often highly sensitive to disturbance.

• **BE DISCRETE WITH FIXED ANCHORS** *Bolts are controversial and are no convenience* – don't place 'em unless they are *really* necessary. Camouflage all anch Remove unsightly slings from rappel stations (better to use steel chain or welded c shuts). Bolts sometimes can be used proactively to protect fragile resources – consult w your local land manager.

• **RESPECT THE RULES** and speak up when other climbers don't. Expect restrictions designated wilderness areas, rock art sites, caves, and to protect wildlife, especially nest birds of prey. *Power drills are illegal in wilderness and all national parks.*

• **PARK AND CAMP IN DESIGNATED AREAS** Some climbing areas require a per for overnight camping.

• **MAINTAIN A LOW PROFILE** Leave the boom box and day-glo clothing at home the less climbers are heard and seen, the better.

• **RESPECT PRIVATE PROPERTY** Be courteous to land owners. Don't climb whe you're not wanted.

• **JOIN THE ACCESS FUND** To become a member, make a tax-deductible donation of $2

The Access Fund
Preserving America's Diverse Climbing Resources
PO Box 17010
Boulder, CO 80308
303.545.6772 • www.accessfund.org